ROUTLEDGE LIBRARY EDITIONS:
EDUCATION

CHILDREN AND LEARNING TO READ

CHILDREN AND LEARNING TO READ

ELIZABETH J. GOODACRE

Volume 114

Routledge
Taylor & Francis Group

LONDON AND NEW YORK

First published in 1971

This edition first published in 2012
by Routledge
2 Park Square, Milton Park, Abingdon, Oxfordshire OX14 4RN

Simultaneously published in the USA and Canada
by Routledge
711 Third Avenue, New York, NY 10017

First issued in paperback 2014

Routledge is an imprint of the Taylor and Francis Group, an informa company

British Library Cataloguing in Publication Data
A catalogue record for this book is available from the British Library

ISBN 13: 978-0-415-69449-0 (volume 114)
ISBN 13: 978-0-415-75103-2 (pbk)

Publisher's Note
The publisher has gone to great lengths to ensure the quality of this reprint but
points out that some imperfections in the original copies may be apparent.

Disclaimer
The publisher has made every effort to trace copyright holders and would
welcome correspondence from those they have been unable to trace.

Children and Learning to Read

by Elizabeth J. Goodacre

LONDON

ROUTLEDGE & KEGAN PAUL

First published in Great Britain 1971
by Routledge and Kegan Paul Ltd
Broadway House
68-74 Carter Lane
London, EC4V 5EL
Printed in Great Britain by
Northumberland Press Ltd
Gateshead

ISBN 0 7100 6969 3 (c)
ISBN 0 710c 6970 7 (p)

The effort expended during this century on research and
experiment in the learning and teaching of reading has been
enormous, as any teacher or research student who ventures
to inquire into the literature of the subject will quickly
discover. Has this area of education really benefited from
this effort? Undoubtedly it has, but it is not easy to say
precisely or quickly what the gains have been. We now
know that learning to read is a very complex process, that
it cannot be usefully separated off from the learning of
other language skills, that individual variations among
children in approach, pace of learning and problems encountered are among the most significant factors. We also
know that skilled teachers are more important than any
particular method.

But skill comes only with sufficient first hand experience,
and experience which has been reflected upon and
augmented by disciplined study. There are very few good
introductions to this complex matter for the student
teacher. I regard Mrs Goodacre's book as among the best I

have seen. It is extremely thorough in its treatment and crisp and penetrating in its judgments. It has the wisdom of experience and scholarship behind it, but remains lucid throughout. It is one of the most reliable guides we have and should be very popular with students in Colleges of Education and with serving teachers concerned to come to closer grips with the perennial problems to be found in this key area of learning.

BEN MORRIS

Contents

CONTENTS

Acknowledgments

I am indebted to the many teachers who during the last decade have completed questionnaires for me and allowed me to observe them and their pupils going about the business of learning to read. From their answers to my queries, I have obtained much valuable insight into the reading process. Also, I should like to acknowledge my debt to those classes of children with whom in my early teaching days I learned how to help children discover this complex skill. They were very patient with my 'trial-and-error' efforts to learn how to teach reading.

I should like to record my appreciation of my husband's patient and persistent encouragement of my abiding interest in this subject of children learning to read, and I must not forget the assistance, usually unintentional, of Katy, Stephen and Sarah, who seem to be growing up inevitably in a 'rich' reading environment!

Finally, I should like to thank Pamela Jacques for the accuracy with which she has typed successive versions of the book's manuscript.

1
Learning theories and the reading process

After the war, there was a justifiable reaction to the 'traditional' way of teaching the basic skills—the instruction of whole classes of children by the imparting of ill-digested lumps of information. Gradually, however, it was realized that children are individuals, each different from the other in attainment and ability. In such circumstances, it is perhaps unreasonable to expect all children to learn in the same way and to progress at the same rate.

Unfortunately, this climate of opinion not only gave rise to an aversion to class instruction, but also to the very idea of the *teaching* of reading. Many teachers are confident that the provision of colourful, interesting reading matter is enough in itself to get children 'hooked on books'. They believe that reading in an active, progressive classroom is a skill which should be caught rather than taught.

However some teachers are beginning to realize that many of their pupils are only struggling towards greater creativity in their work simply because they lack a firm foundation in the basic skill of reading. It is as true about reading as sailing a boat, or driving a car, that one can really enjoy one's proficiency in the skill when one has mastered it sufficiently to be able to forget all about it! Many children cannot carry out project work effectively or follow up their interests because they cannot read the books they really want to read. Being able to read the pre-digested 'baby's food' of the controlled vocabulary reader does not guarantee being able to find out for yourself how jet engines work or how to consult the reference book you need.

Children must master certain specific sub-skills to be able to read widely and intelligently. Roberts (1969) has enumerated thirteen sub-skills which children need to learn ranging from the child learning that visual symbols carry a language message to using a variety of strategies for forming and recognizing unfamiliar polysyllabic words. The child's familiarity with this hierarchy of sub-skills and his ability to make the whole reading process more automatic, effortless and fluent are highly dependent upon his environment. In the school situation this includes not only the reading facilities and provision of the classroom, but the teacher's competence in structuring this learning situation.

Recent research by the writer (Goodacre, 1969) suggests that the courses in colleges of education have emphasized the importance of child psychology rather than curriculum study. As a result, teachers in our schools are possibly more knowledgeable about stages of child development than the tasks involved in learning to read. The competent teacher is the one who knows about both aspects of the situation, and who can match the complexity of the task to the individual child's stage of development—cognitive, physical and emotional.

How we learn

Presented with a new experience, the learner starts to organize the new 'material' and to relate it to his past experience or to construct 'meaning' out of it. The enriching satisfaction of finding 'meaning' is an important factor and we should not underestimate the frustration for young children of undergoing meaningless experiences. Learning

2

to read has this subjective aspect, and is successful and exciting when this personal element of 'meaningfulness' is evident.

However, the learner's individual construction need not be correct or the most appropriate in the situation. A small child familiar with the concept 'rabbit' or 'bunny' from illustrations in his favourite picture book sees a squirrel in the park. Relating this new experience to his store of personal knowledge, he very logically calls out 'Mummy, look at the funny bunny.' It is salutary to us as teachers to remember that the learner makes his insights whatever happens. Our task is to deduce evidence as to how far his constructs about the reading process are relevant or likely to impede his further learning.

Children's verbal mistakes and inaccuracies—the 'schoolboy howler'—are a gold mine of examples of children trying to make sense of the adult world. Listening to children's conversations, observing their drawings and their written expression, teachers and parents can obtain insight into their children's efforts to make sense of experience. For instance, I recall when my eldest daughter had just started at the infant school, she asked me one day rather sadly, why the infants did not have their own flag. After some discussion, I realized that she had thought that *Union* in *Union Jack* was the more familiar word *Junior*.

The vocabulary of learning to read

In the early stages of learning to read, we may have overrated children's grasp of the concepts involved. Jessie Reid (1966) through the use of structured interviews studied five-year-old school beginners' ideas about the business of 'reading'. At the beginning of their schooling, they seemed to lack any specific expectancies of what reading was going to be like as an activity, of what it consisted, or to under-

3

stand the purpose and use of it, and the relationship between reading and writing.

The main problems were related to the children's uncertainty about the *nature* of the material they had to organize. Confusion arose over the difference between the types of material found in books (pictures or printed symbols); types of printed letters (capital or lower case—Kk); the form of letter groupings (e.g. what constituted a word); the relationship between letter groupings and their corresponding sounds in speech. It was evident from Reid's study that these young children had great difficulty in understanding the abstract technical terms which grown-ups use to talk about language and the reading process; e.g. 'word', 'letter', 'sound', etc.

Downing (1969) has carried out a concept attainment experiment into the understanding of the terms 'word' and 'sound' by young children. He concluded that the term 'sound' was even less well understood than 'word', and that young beginners have serious difficulty in understanding the *purpose* of written language. They had only a vague idea of how people read, and particular difficulty in understanding this type of *abstract* linguistic terminology.

Mason (1967) in the United States studied the attitudes of 178 pre-schoolers learning to read and found that most of them thought they could already 'read'. He concluded that 'one of the first steps in learning to read is learning that one doesn't already know how. This seems to be a step in learning to read or in reading readiness which has been neglected...'.

The skill of reading is a highly complex one and those who have studied it have evolved technical terms to describe its processes. Also, the act of reading is itself an abstract convention. As Downing has pointed out the written form of language is 'an artificial two-dimensional product of civilisation'.

Piaget's studies have enabled us to know more about children's cognitive development and to realize that the logic of young children is qualitatively different from that of adults. As Sybil Marshall (1963) has suggested, children are 'not solely adults in the making, but creatures in their own right, as tadpoles differ from mature frogs, or caterpillars from butterflies'. The child's stage of cognitive development may affect the degree to which he can understand the abstract nature of the reading process. However, educationists such as Jerome Bruner (1960) contend that 'the foundations of any subject may be taught to anybody at any age in some form'. In practice, this means teachers knowing about the stages in acquiring the reading skill and being able to accurately match them to children's developmental stages. As yet, this is not a simple task, partly because a great deal of reading research has concentrated on how adults *believe* children learn to read but also because the various methods of teaching reading are based on aspects of adult rather than children's learning patterns.

There are different theories about the learning process each of which contribute towards our understanding of the way children learn. These theories are reflected in the various methods of teaching reading as well as in the process of learning to read. In chapter 3 this relationship between particular reading methods and the various types of learning theories is discussed at some length.

The insight theory of learning

Seeking after meaning in the early stages of learning is usually based on very personal or idiosyncratic ideas. The insight theory of learning is an explanation of the learning process in terms of holding on to an old mental structure and absorbing information into it, until the accumulation of facts refutes it, and necessitates a reorganization of the material. Generalizing and simplifying occur during this

5

reorganization stage, and it is here that inaccuracies or at least inappropriate conclusions can be formulated by the learner. Then, by further use or practice these ideas are built into the learner's mental equipment to be used to structure and make meaning of fresh experiences.

Children do their best to make sense of their schooling including the experience of learning to read. In the process they may jump to conclusions which impede progress. Mr Thomas Wood writing in *The Teacher* (17 January 1969) tells several anecdotes about reading errors by his pupils. One boy read *told* as *blot* and thought *girl* was *ring*. 'At last he assured me that in future he would read from left to right. But it is not easy to change one's habits. For long enough he thought "now" was "cow" and later on he settled for "down".' Another read *bag* for *peg*. 'Why *bag*?' I said. She pointed to the last letter. 'Is that what you look at first?' I inquired. 'Yes' she said. 'And who told you to do that?' 'Oh, it's my own idea' was the reply.

The behaviourist theory

The evidence for this type of explanation comes chiefly from simple learning situations, often involving the use of comparatively uncomplex organisms. It is suggested that learning takes place when the learner wishes to satisfy a particular need, and that actions followed by satisfaction of needs are stamped in, whereas those followed by unsatisfying states generally fail to be learned. Learning is seen as a form of 'conditioning', i.e. an association is built up between a specific response on the part of the learner to one kind of stimulus. In this way, a particular response becomes a matter of habit.

Some educationalists would suggest that after insight occurs, some form of drill or 'conditioning' of this associative type of learning is necessary for the meaning or 'insight' to be preserved. The 'correct' response can die away for lack of repetition, and space of these 'drill' periods and time spent on them are important factors in the attempt to overlearn or make habitual the association one wishes to foster.

In learning golf, tennis or cricket, the learner is shown how to hold his club, bat, etc. and to 'feel' and recall the appropriate body movements of a good shot. Successful performance is in itself rewarding—the self-congratulation of getting it 'right'—and enforces the correct 'feel'. The learner will carry on practising this co-ordination of movement in order to achieve a high level of skill performance. This idea underlies some of the more recent linguistic methods of learning to read where, by the use of linguistically controlled reading materials, children continually encounter words with high frequency strings of letters or letter groupings which have a one-to-one relationship between the symbols and their sounds. Thus they are conditioned to look for this relationship between letters and sounds and think of reading as a relatively simple decoding process.

The perceptual theory

These ideas about learning involve changes in behaviour. To understand fully how behaviour can be changed requires some appreciation of the causes of behaviour and these lie in the perceptual field of the learner. If learning is to take place, there must be changes in how the learner habitually perceives things, and this can be brought about by a process of differentiation. The means of satisfying personal needs exists in the learner's environment. Individuals tend to seek out those circumstances and events which best satisfy these needs. The process of becoming increasingly aware of a range of satisfying factors involves paying closer attention to more and more detail in the environment, i.e. of differentiating it.

7

For instance, if you are at a party and meet a friend and chat, usually you have only a hazy recollection afterwards of what the person was wearing. One is aware of clothing as one factor in the situation but usually it is unnecessary to note details. You can, however, observe much more closely or in the behaviourist's language 'differentiate elements in the field', if there is a need to, or if one has been alerted to do so. We are usually more aware of how strangers at a party are dressed, because observing details of dress can be one way of 'sizing up' a stranger, thus attempting to bring under control unfamiliar aspects of this environment. In learning to read, it may be necessary for teachers to alert pupils to the importance of particular details, e.g. to look more closely at what is the difference between similar letter forms such as *b* and *d*. The experiences of children before coming to school differ greatly in the extent to which the home has encouraged pupils to observe fine differences in perceptual details.

A person behaves not only according to the way in which he perceives the situation, which is not necessarily the situation as it exists objectively, but also according to the way in which he habitually thinks about himself. A person may react in a particular way because he believes he is a better-than-average swimmer, a 'good loser', or a 'family man'. Some children, early in their schooling, long before their teachers may realize it, think of themselves as 'poor' readers and behave accordingly. Unless one appreciates the view the individual holds of himself, much of his behaviour can appear puzzling or perhaps even strange.

The developmental theory

Piaget's work has already been mentioned, but at this point his views are particularly relevant. He views the development of cognitive abilities in the child as a form of adaptation, the result of 'the equilibrium between the action of the organism on the environment on the one hand, and the action of the environment on the organism on the other' (Piaget, 1950). Adaptation is seen as an equilibrium between assimilation and accommodation.

The insight theory suggested that we absorb or assimilate various aspects of the environment in which we exist. The perceptual theory stressed the highly individual and personal nature of this organization of our experience. We absorb new experiences in terms of old constructs and incorporate them in various 'schematas'. However, some experiences resist this treatment. They are so strange and unfamiliar that we are unable to assimilate them. Since then the experiences cannot be interpreted in familiar terms, we ourselves must change, and we modify our patterns of behaviour, accommodating to the environment. In the process of learning, this balance between what is known and what is unknown is not a single occurrence but goes on continuously. The balance shifts as more complex situations are encountered. One has 'insights' but later these are reconstructed.

It is some time before the very young child accumulates sufficient experience about the world and sufficient equilibrium in various fields of experience to form a reasonably stable world of impressions. At birth, and for many months afterwards, there is no 'world' only a disorganized mass of sensations—no sense of self and not-self—as Piaget has written 'the child floats in an *undifferentiated* absolute' (italics added).

Piaget thinks of the child's intelligence as a growing expression of adaptation, first of all, expressed in sensorimotor activity, but later going beyond perception and habit, gradually operating at greater distances and by more complex routes, and becoming both more versatile and reversible. His ideas emphasize the importance of children's thinking starting in action. Children need much experience of manipulating things, but this is not an end in itself. The ultimate stage is formal operations, release from the control of the physical properties of experience, and the performance of action as internalized thought.

In learning to read, this probably means that at the beginning stages children should have plenty of opportunity of exploring through touch the letter forms, of matching visual images and their word forms, and listening to and experimenting with different sounds including the sound components of words. Children probably need to be helped to reach the last stage of formal operations, and for reading this would include being able to read at a rate related to the nature of the material, to absorb the total meaning of the passage and not just the meaning of individual words, and to use both context and word recognition clues to read unfamiliar words.

Piaget has suggested that maturity of thinking is achieved in four stages. These are the *sensori-motor* stage which explains most of the action of a child up to two years of age; *pre-operational* which accounts for the beginnings of thinking from the ages of two to seven years; the stage of *concrete* operations from the ages of seven to eleven years; and lastly, the mature level of thinking, *formal and operational*, which takes place beyond eleven years. Although research generally supports Piaget's ideas, evidence suggests that the ages mentioned by him correspond more to mental than chronological ages. Also, some people have interpreted Piaget as meaning that all our thought after reaching the teens is at the operational level. Adults tend to aspire to the condition of operational thinking, but there is plenty of evidence to suggest that if the task is very new or perhaps very difficult, then the individual will find himself having to move through some of these preliminary stages.

Learning how to teach reading

In this context, it is interesting to consider how teachers learn about the teaching of reading. Recently the professional preparation of teachers in relation to teaching reading has come under some criticism. Studying the respective views of the Colleges of Education and head teachers, it does seem that the latter are expecting the colleges to turn out a finished product, fully equipped and ready for active service. However, a great deal of the theoretical aspects of the teaching of reading—the more abstract ideas about the reading process—may only begin to make sense to teachers after several years of practical experience in the classroom.

This is especially true in respect to recognizing and being able to help the potentially slow reader. Generally speaking, most teachers have themselves learned to read very quickly and easily. Few seem to have experienced any persistent difficulty with reading in their childhood, or for that matter can even recall actually learning to read. Asked about this, teachers have often said to me that as a child they 'just read'—one day they were not, and the next they were reading. Many teachers, therefore, may have little personal insight into the difficulty and complexity of the process for some children.

In order to understand the reading process, it may be necessary for most teachers (a) to be alerted to specific instances of children's difficulties, and given opportunities to recognize and help certain types of readers; (b) to handle and use for themselves the teaching apparatus and material used by children at the *concrete* stage of learning the skill; (c) to read and collect information from research about the stages of learning to read of which they may have little insight; i.e. to differentiate levels of difficulty within the complex process.

Through exploration by means of the sense of touch,

smell, sight and hearing, children gain experience and look for consistencies in it. Usually it is the most striking aspect of the situation, which tends to be considered. Only later, more than one aspect can be considered and logical deductions made possible.

Considering the state of reading research, in some ways, we are still at the stage of early infancy, since much of the research has concentrated on single factors—some of them of a particularly concrete nature—failed to distinguish between conflicting principles, and to examine less familiar alternative ideas.

For instance, most readers will be familiar with the experiments in i.t.a.—the use of the initial teaching or Augmented Roman alphabet which introduces a high degree of phoneme/grapheme correspondence by using additional symbols. For young children for a limited period such consistency may be useful when they are at the stage of considering one aspect at a time and because of home background are relatively unfamiliar with print. However, there are other types of 'signalling devices' which can be used; e.g. *Words in Colour* (Gattegno), *Colour Story Reading* (Jones); *Diacritical Marking* (Fry). Such devices may be effective with particular types of children.

For a decade, reading research, at least in this country, has been concentrating primarily on one aspect of the reading situation—the *medium* in which children learn to read. This is essentially a concrete aspect. It is of interest to note that the most recent and thought-provoking work is in the following three areas:

(a) the study of children's oral reading errors or 'miscues', e.g. Clay (1966 and 1969); Biemiller (1968); Goodman (1969).

(b) the exploration of children's concepts of reading —what 'reading' involves and their understanding of 'technical terms', e.g. Reid (1966); Downing (1969).

(c) the formulation of theories of reading based on the idea of reading as a continuing process rather than a 'suddenly arrived at' skill. The integration of language skills and content, means that reading is increasingly being seen as a tool for mining all subjects, and therefore a facet of an individual's total growth, e.g. Chall (1969).

In research we seem at last to be escaping from the limitations of the concrete stage of thought, and from preoccupations with *medium* and *materials* and to be looking beyond these physical attributes of the reading situation. Possibly reading research, as an expanding field of knowledge, is moving into its more formal and operational stages.

2

Stages in cognitive growth and reading

Time span of learning to read

The literature on the teaching of reading is full of references to when a child *should* start to learn to read, but there is less evidence available as to the earliest age at which children are able to successfully start to learn. This is because the question of 'reading readiness' is closely connected with ideas about 'readiness' in general and what 'learning to read' constitutes at these early stages.

To start with the first point, between the wars educationists were greatly concerned with the respective contributions of environmental and hereditary factors. Concentration upon the importance of maturation in the learning process led to the type of educational climate in which it was considered morally wrong to push a child—it was considered desirable for children to be left alone until they were ready. Children would learn to read eventually, as they learn to walk or talk and the process could not be hurried. In the light of these educational tenets, it is not surprising to find that a particular study (Morphett and Washburne, 1931) assumed importance out of all proportion to its worth. With its suggestion that children could *not* be successfully *taught* to read until the mental age of six and a half, it provided ammunition for the 'wait and leave well alone' school of thought.

A series of experiments by Gates (1937) produced evidence that the age of beginning *systematic* reading instruction was relative to the learning conditions existing; the more favourable conditions (e.g. small classes, competent teachers, appropriate reading materials) the earlier beginning was possible. This evidence was largely ignored and in reading literature the idea of a mental age of six and a half was widely accepted as a criterion of 'reading readiness'.

The second point that should be considered is what is understood by 'systematic reading instruction'. If this is understood to mean introducing the child to phonetic analysis in order to enable him to learn to associate sound and symbol and develop an understanding of phoneme/ grapheme correspondence, then a certain degree of mental maturity may be necessary to achieve this particular reading task. 'Cracking the code' as it is sometimes called, is certainly a necessary stage in learning to read if children are to be able to unlock words for themselves and progress on their own. In considering favourable learning conditions, one must include the ability of the teacher to simplify reading tasks and to produce a sequence in their introduction. To achieve phonetic analysis, children need not only to have had considerable auditory experience (some of it obtained in the home), but also to understand what is wanted of them; that is, to be able to analyse and to distinguish parts within familiar 'wholes'. Also, the review of skills which have been introduced is essential. The key to such teaching is *diagnosis*, which then becomes an integral part of systematic instruction.

Since the war a series of sociologically orientated studies confirmed that achievement in school is the combined result of innate ability and of environment, and this emphasis upon the combined effect of home and school has led to re-assessments of the idea of 'reading readiness'; these have included evidence of children learning to 'read' well below the mental age of six and a half.

It is of interest in the light of the above paragraphs on 'learning conditions' to find that most of the young children who attempted 'reading' at a mental age of four or less either learned individually or in small groups, and were motivated to learn because of the example of an older child in the family or strong parental interest in reading (e.g. Suton, 1964; Pleassas and Oakes, 1964; Durkin, 1964). Books and reading materials were part of the child's environment from a very early age and reading both a familiar form of entertainment and a source of pride. However, where the subjects were retarded five-year-olds (mental age four years), it was noticeable that although they managed to remember a small sight vocabulary (recognize a certain number of words), they failed to make progress when they reached the more complex stages (e.g. Davidson, 1931).

Examples of individual children who have started to learn to read at a very early age have been cited by Fowler (1962) and by Lynn (1963). Both researchers taught their own children to recognize words when the children were nearly three, Fowler's child learning 250 words whilst Lynn taught his daughter a hundred words. It should be noted that both the children quoted were the researcher's own child, were girls, and had high intelligence quotients —their mental ages being three and a half and four. Both children after periods of nine and three months respectively, developed resistance to the situation. Lynn's daughter six months later was only able to recognize about one word in three, suggesting that at this early age children experience difficulty not so much in being able to see and distinguish the features of the words, but in formulating means to discriminate one word from another, and probably also, in transferring the words from short-term immediate *memory* into long-term permanent storage.

Going up the mental age scale, a study by Bruce (1964) of

children (mental age five plus to nine plus), provides evidence about the development in children of the ability to make a simple phonetic analysis of the spoken word. Bruce found that children (mental age five) had little appreciation of the relationship between sound and word, particularly that they were exclusive categories. As Downing has suggested, young children at the beginning of their schooling are probably not clear about the relationship between the concept of the written word and the units in speech, and what the teacher means by a more technical use of the word 'sound'. There was, however, a gradual progress towards accurate phonetic analysis in the course of which the children came to understand that (a) words and sounds were different concepts but they were interrelated; (b) began to understand what was wanted of them to carry out 'phonetic analysis'—e.g. S-T-AND, say the word left when the middle sound is taken away, or first as in J-AM, or last as in TEN-T; (c) were able to understand differences of position—first, last, middle sounds; (d) overcame the cohesiveness of the word sound pattern in their experience. A mental age of seven plus seemed to be the level of development at which the abilities involved in this task were sufficiently developed to ensure a level of success. However, the types of errors being made at mental age nine suggested that even at this stage of their cognitive development children were still not clear about the *position* of *sounds* within *words* and how to break up words into constituent sounds. It should be noted that up to mental age nine there was a difference between children according to the school they attended and the school's approach to the teaching of reading. The school which stressed phonic instruction (teaching of 'letter sounds') from the beginning had the highest mean score based on success in the task. Did these children find the task easier because their teachers had already alerted them to the importance of letters and their sounds?

Perhaps children should not be considered backward in reading much before a mental age of nine, since teachers are very familiar with the slow child who seems to make a spurt in the first year juniors; i.e. mental age six to seven. At this stage the slow child seems to begin to understand and benefit from systematic instruction, particularly in applying phonetic generalizations to their slowly accumulated sight vocabulary. Using this knowledge not only can they sound out unfamiliar words, but also use contextual clues to determine the appropriate letter sound (e.g. which vowel variation to use in the word and sentence context). By reason of the child's increasing experience of print he is conditioned to seeing letter combinations in written words. He expects certain letter groupings, and very gradually learns to distinguish certain speech parts or units as distinct sounds (e.g. units such as the *phoneme* = the smallest speech unit; or the *morpheme* = the smallest linguistic unit to have meaning— prefixes and suffixes).

Studies such as those described suggest that the process of beginning to learn to read can broadly be associated with a *mental age* range of approximately three to nine. How does this correspond with the stages in children's thinking?

Piaget's stages in relation to reading

Sensori-motor: The child at this earliest stage has difficulty in distinguishing between himself and his environment. He learns what is not self by exploration and through his physical senses. Life is very much of the here and now. When an object is out of sight, it no longer exists. One writer (Goldman, 1957) has suggested that: '... it is this lack of stability and continuity which makes this period rather like a slow-motion film. Pictures of the world are seen separately in succession but there is no fusion or experience on the whole.'

However, gradually events build up expectations of regular happenings. In language, sound patterns stand not only for objects present, but also for absent objects. *If* books are present in the environment, they are there as objects which can be handled, sucked and chewed, or someone in the child's environment shows how they can be used—pages are turned, objects represented in two-dimensional form identified and named. Three articles in *Books for Your Children* written by observant mothers provide delightful insights into the use of books at this early stage. I can but quote in detail since Mrs Wood's words (Autumn issue, 1966) so accurately describe the combination of physical exploration and experiments with sounds:

Ten Months: The cloth book *The Big Book of Many Things* is easier for her to handle than her first one. *Baby's Book of Toys* (both Bancroft). The pictures mean nothing but handling the books gives great pleasure. Tiny cloth books do not seem to appeal, the bigger the better.

No satisfying board book to be found. Taking up her enthusiasm for dogs I have found *My Picture Book of Dogs*, published by Bancroft. It measures 12in.×10in., has DOGS in red letters 2in. high, a glossy cover with the portrait of a wolf hound on one side, golden retriever on the other. It is a great success. She turns it over and over and loves best the dog on the back (a golden retriever lives in the house opposite). She croons over this in the same way as she 'loves' her golliwog. No other animal book evokes the same response. Some, with glamourised photographs merged with background (e.g. roe-deer fawn) are merely playthings to be chewed (especially the plastic ring bindings).

One Year: The dog book still the experience of the day but she enjoys playing with *The Big Book of Many Things*. turns over the pages haphazardly 'talking' to colours or shapes, handling the book affords satisfaction. Fifteen Months: The dog book has taken over from *The Book of Many Things* as a plaything. Though difficult to handle, it is still interesting and is treated with respect....

Where's My Baby? by H. A. Rey (Chatto and Windus) is great fun, she has quickly learned the trick of lifting the flap. We vary this with *Anybody At Home?* The favourite is bees leaving the hive because of improvised finger movements and zzzzzzzzz noise which she joins in.

Sixteen Months: *The Story of Little Black Sambo* by Helen Bannerman (Chatto and Windus) has gradually become *the* favourite. From turning over the pages quickly to reach the tigers going 'round and round' the tree (as in round and round the garden—a favourite finger play), we have added more sound effects and first she is completely absorbed, growls with the tigers and throws up hands with Sambo quite spontaneously. What a marvellous book, exactly the right size (the fascination of *big* books has waned). The drama out of dressing, eating, undressing and eating, life itself to a baby....

This description shows very clearly the way this particular child was making meaningful associations; picture of a dog like the dog she knew, round and round the tree as in the familiar finger play, joining in to make the bee's buzzing sound, exploring size in the shapes of books. Activity and exploration, and note the active role of the mother!

Through such experiences the child in the book-conscious home develops recognition of two-dimensional, pictorial representations of familiar objects. The idea may develop that pictorial and written symbols (letter forms) are both means of communication, but different. Some children may even realize that written symbols can represent familiar objects. They are able to recognize different words, usually identifying them by their length, overall shape or configuration, or the form of beginning or end letters. The size of this 'sight' vocabulary is likely to be limited by their experience, their interest, and memory development. However, probably for most children at this stage 'reading' is interpreting and getting meaning from pictures.

Pre-Operational: Piaget divides this into two phases, the transductive period, when memory becomes possible as the abstraction from action to thought occurs, and the later intuitive phase leading into the operational stage. With the development of language, the object is symbolized, however crudely, and gradually is retained as sensory imagery. Amongst pre-schoolers symbolism is used extensively in play. The yellow centres of daisies remind one of the yolk of one's fried egg at breakfast, and the daisy heads are served up on plastic tea plates as breakfast in the Wendy house. It is just as simple to accept that squiggles on paper are *eggs* or *cornflakes* as well.

In the early stages of collecting word patterns, length may be a useful way of discriminating one word from another; *dog* is a little word; *aeroplane* is a long one. What happens when words are of similar length? Children probably then look for other peculiarities or characteristics to aid discrimination and these may be highly specific or idiosyncratic; e.g. 'I know that says *monkey* because the end looks like his tail'; '*laugh* looks like a clown's mouth, have you noticed?' Words are seen as groupings of letters with space either side and one result of this is that children begin to notice beginning and end letters of words (Marchbanks and Levin, 1965). Middle letters on the other hand are embedded in the word and in the early stages there is often confusion regarding the sequence of letters in the 'middle'. This is noticeable with certain spelling mistakes, which sort themselves out in time. Research at this early stage of word recognition suggests that children concentrate solely on the visual aspect of words, and have great difficulty in switching to sounding words, or in matching the visual presentation of letter combinations or patterns of dots and dashes with letter sounds or tapped out rhythms.

At the *transductive stage*, experience is increasing and so generalizations can be made, but they are often wildly inaccurate, since the child reasons transductively from particular to particular. Piaget has suggested that children during this phase are unable to see more than one or two factors in a situation and cannot reverse their thought or test if it is true conversely. It is therefore not altogether surprising to find children guessing *they* for *yellow*, and not being able to use the context as a clue at the same time. Gradually with familiarity with print, particular letter combinations are expected and 'little words' may even be seen in long words. Visually words are more and more accurately observed and eventually seen as total configurations and possibly overall shape does become an important clue. At this stage, however, it is probably extremely difficult for children to break up the slowly acquired *sound* pattern of words in order to relate phonemes to graphemes, or even to hear and distinguish morphemes.

During the *intuitive stage*, the child has insufficient experience to contradict the evidence of his senses, but towards the end of the stage, he begins to question the evidence of his eyes. He tries to make sense of the whole complex business of experience to get the true and functional meaning of factors such as length, number, etc. The bright child, the one whose powers of making generalizations are developing, soon abstracts the useful information that beginning and end letters of words have corresponding speech sounds, thus discovering for himself the principle of phonetic analysis. In school this often seems to stem from children noticing each other's Christian names. 'Jack and Jim start the same way.' Karen says, 'Look, Kevin's name begins with *that* as well.' Some teachers make displays of objects beginning with the same letter or encourage children to collect words beginning with a particular letter. When a bright child brings *ginger* and *garage* and says pointing to the beginning letter, 'Of course, this says two different things in these two words,' he has shown not only that he is using the concept 'word', but that he has realized certain letters have more than one sound. It may be some time before he realizes the reverse of this, that similar 'sounds' (phonemes) can be produced by different letter combinations; e.g. *seat, meet,* etc.

Concrete phase: By this stage the two important principles of reversibility and conservation become available thereby making the development from simple word recognition to self-help possible. The child has sufficient experience to be able (a) to classify objects and experiences, separate like and unlike, to generalize more or less accurately (e.g. two sounds of letter '*g*'; three sounds of '*y*' depending on its position); this involves seeing groups classified within other larger groups—e.g. terrier is a dog, dog is an animal —letters are in words, words are in sentences (what is *a*?), capital and small case letters are both letters; (b) to seriate —to grasp the idea of an ordered and true sequence; e.g. first, second, etc. end, middle, and so realize the importance of sequence, order and position; e.g. *was, saw; bad, dad*.

The child gradually learns to ignore irrelevant variations; e.g. differences in shape of letters related to script or type; sounds related to accent. He learns from experience that letters can produce different sounds, but the usual or 'correct' pronunciation is determined by inclusion in a word. He learns to deal with more than one factor simultaneously. For instance, variation in the vowel sound (long or short) may lead to the reader trying internally several pronunciations very rapidly until by trial and error the right 'fit' is reached which is in line with the signals from the contextual clues. Recent research suggests that this trial and error, re-reading and re-phrasing may have to be done orally in order for the child to obtain sufficient auditory 'feed back'.

MacKinnon (1959) observed children closely when they were learning to read and concluded that spontaneous re-reading occurred either when the child recognized that they had made a word recognition error in the light of the context or when they had achieved successful word recognition of each word but had not got the total meaning. This behaviour was especially true in the early stages. MacKinnon's findings were supported by research by Clay (1966) who hypothesized that in the process of correcting their own errors, children seemed gradually to become aware of what they were doing and were able to verbalize it. With some children, Clay noticed there was a gradual transition from finger pointing (following the context word by word with the finger) to what could be described as 'voice pointing' or the familiar word-by-word type of reading. This 'pointing' seemed to serve an important function in the early stages, as it aided the child in making the one-to-one correspondence between the printed and the spoken word. Practice in using the skill eventually led to a lighter stress on individual words and finally to a greater dependence on phrasing and grouping words, or what a great many teachers describe as 'fluent reading'. With fast learners this transition was so rapid as to be almost unnoticed.

Passing out of the concrete stage, children operate at a *formal* level, using their skill in a flexible and mature manner; e.g. they adjust their reading rate to the level of difficulty of the reading matter, and they mentally organize what is read so that they obtain an overall meaning.

3
Methods of teaching reading

The main methods of teaching reading are usually understood to be the alphabetic, the phonic, the 'whole-word' or 'look-and-say' and the sentence method. However, the growing emphasis upon the importance of individual differences has led to the discussion in the literature on method of two approaches—the 'language experience' approach and 'individualized reading'. This chapter therefore concludes with a description of these two approaches and outlines some of the advantages and disadvantages of using such approaches.

The alphabetic method

By this method it is assumed that familiarity with the *form* and *names* of *letters* will help children to recognize and pronounce words. By constant repetition of the letter-names (e.g. 'dee-oe-gee'), this spelling out of words will enable the learner to become familiar not only with the form and name of individual letters but also become accustomed to meeting certain letter-strings or letter clusters, the component parts of many words. Generally, the main emphasis was laid on the recognition of new words rather than the grasp of meaning. To this extent this method relies heavily on the conditioning aspect of the learning process.

The difficulty with isolating and discussing particular methods is that one never knows exactly how far such methods are successful in their ostensible aims and how far they may inadvertently be teaching other helpful sub-skills. Also, as Diack has pointed out in his book *In Spite of the Alphabet* (1965) it is hard to tell how far specific methods are differentiated one from another. It is not very far from teaching the *names* of the letters to teaching their *sounds*. As Diack notes 'of alphabetic and phonic methods it can indeed be said that "thin partitions do their bounds divide"'. Children make their own deductions and in the case of teaching the letter names, it is quite possible for the bright child to realize that there is a fairly close correspondence between the name of the letter and its sound for *some* of the letters. This can help them to realize that there is a code involved in learning to read, and to pronounce initial letters which can be helpful for trying to read unfamiliar words.

Durrell (1968) has suggested that for all the consonants (the letters of the alphabet with the exception of the vowels *a, e, i, o, u*) letter-names, except for the letters *h, q, w* and *y,* contain their phonemes or sounds plus an extraneous vowel, and the names of the vowels are the 'long' sound *ae, ee, ie, oe, ue.* In the names of the 'long-e' letters; e.g. *b, c, d, g, p, t, v, z* (this last in American though not in English), the phoneme comes in front of the vowel in the letter name—*b-ee, s-ee,* etc.; to say these letters the child uses exactly the same speech mechanisms as in giving the 'sounds'. The names of the 'short-e' letter, e.g. *f, l, m, n, s, x* —have a similar value, with the phoneme following the vowel in the name; e.g. *eh-l, eh-m.* The names *r, k,* and *y,* also contain their phonemes or letter sounds. Durrell considers that the close association between name and sound in 22 of the 26 letters is a great help for word recognition and pronunciation. He cites work which showed that when the letter-name was known, the sound of the letter was easier to learn.

With these considerations in mind, it is interesting to note that in studies of children who learned to read before going to school, interest in and concern with letters was found to be positively associated with early success in reading (Durkin's studies, 1964, etc.). The American Government spent an enormous amount of money on a research programme called First Grade Reading Programmes which produced as the most important finding the fact that no one method was superior to any other and that the really important factor was the understanding and competence of the teacher. However, another interesting finding was that the best single predictor of success in the beginning stages of learning to read was a test of the letter-names (Bond-Dykstra, 1967). Indeed, work by Hillerich (1967) has suggested that knowledge of the letter-names at the beginning of schooling is a better predictor of later reading achievement than even the scores of a specially designed reading readiness test.

However, such findings should not be interpreted as indicating a causal relationship, or that it is therefore necessary that children must be taught the letter-names in order to read. In trying to discover how children learn to read, Muehl (1962) found that children who were taught letter-names experienced an initial handicap in identifying nonsense syllables because, in trying to identify the printed symbol, the child had to pass through an intermediate step of saying the letter-name before he arrived at the beginning sound of the word. Certainly, many teachers prefer not to teach the letter-names, or to postpone this until after the child has acquired an extensive sight vocabulary.

Porter and Popp (1967) prior to development of a teaching device called an alpha-board made many attempts to teach school beginners the letter-names. They used Lotto-

27

type games, card sorting and spelling games, stories about the letters, and 'alphabet' songs. Their efforts were largely unsuccessful, but their comments are useful. Children could find a letter named by the researcher more easily at this stage than they could name the letters themselves. The researchers came to the conclusion that the popular 'alphabet song' can lead to very serious confusions and that the alphabetical sequence, particularly at the beginning of the alphabet, generated auditory and visual discrimination difficulties; e.g. *b* and *d*. They concluded that letter-names were really 'nonsense syllables' to most of these young children, but a useful concept was to teach the visible difference between *letters* and *words*. Certainly letters whose names are very similar should not be taught at the same time, as this is much too confusing for young children.

It has been suggested that the explanation for the high relationship between knowledge of letter-names and reading success is that a test of letter-names is really a very crude or naïve intelligence test. It measures such things as (a) the child's exposure to print; (b) the amount of attention he has received at home; (c) his ability to retain knowledge gained from these experiences with letters; (d) his ability to pay attention and look closely at letter forms. A recent review of the various readiness measures for predicting reading achievement has suggested that the child's ability to 'attend', to look closely and see differences, and his level of oral development and therefore use of language concepts are factors in reading readiness which need to be more closely investigated. Chall (1967) has also drawn attention to the importance of letter knowledge as a clue to the child's cognitive development.

The alphabet is a code, an abstraction, perhaps the first that a child learns (and one that is valued because adults value it). Pointing to and naming a letter, or writing a letter, at an early age is quite different from pointing to or drawing a picture of a cat, a truck, or a tree. The child who can identify or reproduce a letter engages in symbolic representation, to borrow a phrase from Jerome Bruner, while the child who is working with a picture of an actual object engages in iconic representation. When the child engages in symbolic representation, he is already practicing a *higher form of intellectual behaviour* (my italics).

Work by Wheelock and Silvaroli (1967) suggests that young children can be trained to make instant responses of recognition to the capital letters. What is of interest though is that the training in letter recognition appeared to be of most benefit to the children who came from lower socio-economic homes. Matching letter shapes, possibly even naming the letters (but not in alphabetic order) are means of helping the young child to pay attention to the letters, and this must be of help in observing differences in the *order* of letters in words and the use of letters as clues to beginning sounds of words. We know from the study of Marchbanks and Levin (1965) that specific letters formed the most salient cues in children's word identification. The 'standing out' quality of first and last letters seemed to be related to the fact that each is isolated on one side by white space, whereas middle letters are 'lost' in the word form. Thus, print and words themselves draw the child's attention to the importance of beginning and end letters, i.e. the positioning of letters as well as their shape.

It has been suggested that the alphabetic method is of limited usefulness for reading words and sentences, and it has been long held that it is a mechanical and difficult method, and that at its heyday it produced uninteresting reading material; e.g. *the cat sat on the mat*. However, we are now at the stage of considering *how* methods can be adapted to children's cognitive development. The teacher's ability to work out means of simplifying the learning task for each child, building on whatever information or knowledge the pupil already possesses, is an important factor.

We know that *some* children will, by the time of beginning school, be interested in letters and how they differ one from another (some boys can easily distinguish letter forms, even names, from experience with car number plates, or engine numbers). In talking about letters, they must be called something and probably at *this* stage their names are the most appropriate term. As Reid (1966) has pointed out children go through a process of differentiating symbols from pictures, numbers from letters, and letters from words. As she says, later they come to realize that there are different kinds of letters—capital and lower case, and different kinds of words (e.g. the confusing use of the term *name* for children's names, letter-names, etc.). However it seems fairly obvious that very young children need plenty of experience in playing with *letter forms*, so as to become familiar with their shape and learn their correct orientation; e.g. which way round. Tracing round wooden letters, feeling cut-out letter forms in felt stuck on to paper or card; matching small case letters in in-set trays; matching capital letters—possibly matching capital and lower case letters; making familiar words on felt boards from cellograph letters, or plastigraph letters on plastigraph boards. Some teachers use a system whereby children act out letter shapes so the memory of the shape is firmly implanted.

The phonic method

In this method, the *sounds* of letters are substituted for the letter-names.

Originally, the sounds of individual letters were taught but mainly in the last decade, linguists have pointed out that letter sounds are never produced singly but in the context of words, and that usually the positioning of the letter determines its particular sound. If individual letters are sounded there is a tendency for *uh* to be added, so that one gets the distorted pronunciation *huh*, *ruh*, and *guh*. When the sounds of individual letters are 'blended' or synthesized, one gets the word *bat* sounding more like *barter*, which can be very confusing to some children.

Certain educationists have suggested a more suitable synthesis is achieved by beginning with a consonant-vowel combination (since consonants cannot be accurately sounded except with a vowel), such as *c-at* or *ca-t*. Durrell (1968) favours the former rather than the latter practice. He cites a study of the abilities of school beginners to read unfamiliar words in which it was found that even those children who were taught the *ca-t* approach could get from *cap* to *nap* with greater ease than from *man* to *map*. There are not all that number of three-letter words with medial short vowels in the ordinary child's vocabulary, but *at* is a fairly reliable generalization in comparison with *ca* which can say different things in *came*, *call*, *car*, *care*, *catch*. Durrell claims that in most of the 225 phonograms from which stem many of the words familiar to young children, the vowel is stable; relatively few change vowel sounds with the *initial* consonant, in the way that the *ant* phonogram changes in the word *want*. Then, of course, the same sound cluster can be spelled in different ways, e.g. the *air* sound more often than not being spelled *ear*, *are*, *air*. However, this may not be such a difficulty for children when they are *reading* since context can help to indicate the pronunciation if the word is already in the child's oral vocabulary.

Problems and controversies have, and still do, abound in the teaching of phonics. Probably the one that must be dealt with first is the difference in *approach* to the teaching of phonics, since many of the criticisms in the past levelled at phonics as a method, in practice, relate to the approach adopted by the teacher. One type of approach is to introduce children to pictures of an *a*pple, *e*lephant, *I*ndian, *o*strich (not bird!), and *u*mbrella, so that the children are familiar with the short vowel sounds through this use of key pictures. These key pictures carry a phonic clue which provides information about the beginning letter's sound and not its name. This is followed by more pictures of a *squirrel, monkey, fox, rabbit, goat, nest, bear, tiger, pig* and *dog,* to illustrate the more common sounds of the consonants *s, m, f, r, g, n, b, t, f* and *d.* Once the short vowel sounds and the sounds of these ten consonants are learned they are blended together, first into syllables (*su, so, si, se, sa*), then into words (*sun, sob, sit, set, sat*). These initial exercises are followed by reading matter of the following sort:

Sam sat in the sun
The sun is good for Sam (Hay and Wingo, 1948).

As can be seen the procedure tends to be a deductive one. That is, beginning with generalizations about the sounds of letters (which may or may not use *picture* clues of objects which may or may not be familiar to the individual child), these are then applied to the pronunciation of specific syllables and words. It tends to be a *synthetic* process in that it initially concentrates on parts of words which are later combined into whole words. As with the confusion between letter-names of similar sound or letters which are similar in form, it may be difficult for some children to differentiate between similar word parts and three-letter words, i.e. words of similar length.

Sometimes in this use of phonics, reading of interesting material is delayed until the pupils have achieved a high degree of mastery of the 'sounds' and are competent at word building. Critics of this way of teaching phonics instance the difficulties of combining letter sounds into meaningful words by synthesizing, which may lead to awkward articulation and a slower rate of reading. Although the training or conditioning element in the approach can lead to the discovery of phonic generalizations, it is not yet clear how far these expectations can be substantiated in ordinary classroom reading materials, as distinct from the specially designed phonic readers; i.e. what degree of transfer operates.

Also, how valid are these phonic rules?

Clymer (1963) and Bailey (1967) found the two-vowel rule 'the first vowel says its name, the second is usually silent' sometimes stated as 'when two vowels go out walking, the first does all the talking', to be more often wrong than right. They found that others among these so-called 'rules' lack desirable dependability. Programming a computer to spell, some researchers devised 111 vowel rules and 92 consonant rules, but the computer only managed to spell correctly half the 17,000 words demanded of it.

Along with the development of 'sight' methods in the late nineteen-twenties in America went a 'new' method of teaching the letter sounds called *intrinsic*, or *incidental* phonics. By this approach the pupil learned a small sight vocabulary of words (words recognized on sight), usually personally meaningful, and then began to compare these words for similarities and thus to extract from the experience valid phonic generalizations; e.g. when a child knows *my*, *mother*, *must* and *me*, or *baby*, *big* and *baker*, he is ready to make generalizations regarding the sounds of the consonants *m* and *b*. Then as more words become familiar, more generalizations can be made about the sounds associated with other letters or letter groupings. This particular way of progressing in phonics can be termed *inductive* or *analytic*, because specific words are used to discover a generalization regarding the sounds of letters, and whole words are analysed to identify and find recurring letters and their associated sounds. Teachers using this approach play the familiar games 'I Spy' and 'I Went

33

Shopping' (I bought *butter*, *bananas* and *beef*); they encourage children to collect words beginning with the same sound; list the children's names under the same beginning sound; make displays of objects beginning with the same sound; have children sort and classify toys or small objects beginning with similar but different sounds; e.g. *v* and *f*, or *t* and *f*—difference between voiced and voiceless consonants, between two voiceless consonants. When a child making his own list of words beginning with the consonant *g* comes to the teacher with *ginger* and says it does not begin the same way as the previous word *game*, he has discovered for himself that certain letters have more than one sound, and he may be able to go on after this insight to discover that *c* has two sounds, but *y* has three, and the vowels have many. The last of these generalizations may not be quite the problem adults have considered it, because one researcher has demonstrated that one can get on quite well in reading when dashes are substituted for vowels!

McCullough (1968) writing on balanced programmes has stressed the importance of achieving a balance between teacher guidance and pupils not only discovering but also *using* generalizations about letters and their sounds.

> The child who must do something with what he has learned learns it better because he knows he will have to use it, and he learns it better because he does use it. If the child who has discovered the sound represented by the letter *m* by means of the teacher's models, *milk* and *man*, then has to record his own induction with his own models (such as *mouse* and *match*, which he chooses), he will remember what he has learned better and will have a record from which to retrieve it if he forgets it.

Children can discover a lot of things for themselves about words and their sounds, as they experiment with a word's *head*, *body* and *tail*, rearranging and twisting them to suit their fancy. This follows on easily from such commercially produced games as 'Jumbled bodies' or 'Misfits'. *Pan* can be turned into *fan*, *fan* into *fat*, and *bill* into *bell*, or he can try to make new words out of old ones such as making *star* turn into *rats*, or by adding a letter make a *can* into a *cane*, but the effects are limited and usually this word play appeals most to the bright child who studies the structure, changes it and experiments with it in a trial-and-error way.

It should be noted that *phonics* is a methed of applying what we know about the study of speech (phonetics) to the reading process and, as such, it involves bringing into play not only the auditory and visual senses, but the ability to combine these two sensory modes of thought. *Phonetics* on the other hand is concerned with classification, description and articulation of the *sounds of speech* and there is a means by which one symbol can represent one sound (International Phonetic Alphabet) but this is not the traditional alphabet. Pitman's i.t.a. or the Augmented Roman alphabet endeavours to produce a symbol for each sound, and so ensure phoneme/grapheme correspondence; one symbol for each sound. It is useful to make this distinction between phonics and phonetics, as writers, particularly linguists such as Fries are conscious of the confusion in the literature on reading methods between the two terms.

The word method

The difficulty with categorizing methods and trying to describe them briefly is that one is tempted continually to describe them historically in order to place them in some sort of perspective and to cover the many criticisms or qualifications which can be made by the informed reader. Hunter Diack in his book *In Spite of the Alphabet* does this in a brilliant *tour de force*, and the reader unfamiliar with this historical survey of reading methods is recommended to read it for elaboration of the points being made in this chapter.

As reading research at various times concentrates on different aspects of the reading process, so different methods emphasize different factors in the process, and as a method becomes more acceptable one sees a hardening of its new and valuable 'insight' into the reading process, into rigid dogma which usually justifies teaching techniques as soulless and ill thought out as the 'new' method was intended to change.

The word method or 'whole-word' or 'look-and-say' way of teaching reading stresses the word and not the letter-name or sound, and has been used as a means of trying to make the reading process more meaningful to children. At least this is the intention and in some ways the popularity or the revival of word methods has provided evidence of the realization by teachers and educationists that the *letter* methods can become boring and meaningless for children if taken to the extreme. In the word methods, it is thought that children's attention can be drawn to an element which is already familiar through the child's speech. Children will see the difference between words on the basis of length and the shape or configuration of the words, and then easily be able to recognize words using such clues. By using words familiar to the child, that is, in the child's own oral vocabulary, it would be possible to get away from the difficult-to-transfer learning situation of phonic word building and blending, and the spelling units of the alphabetic method. Thus children would be more highly motivated to read, and not bored by the 'delayed reading' element which can exist with the use of letter methods, e.g. the synthetic (building up) approach rather than analytic (analysing from known words).

It is useful to distinguish between 'whole-word' and 'look-and-say' methods. Using the former it is possible to associate picture and 'name', that is pictorial representation and the word which stands for it, so that the child is conditioned to accept that the image and the symbol of the word are related. Similarly, objects in the environment can be labelled. This is usually only possible for nouns, and difficulties of interpretation and language experience interfere when it comes to concrete or pictorial representation of verbs, adverbs, adjectives, etc. For this reason 'look-and-say' becomes a means by which the teacher or the adult can tell what the particular word says. As Flesch (1955), a bitter critic of the word method, has insisted, it is in certain circumstances a crude form of conditioning.

> It goes straight back to Pavlov and his famous salivating dogs ... It was not long before the conditioned reflex psychologists ... found out that Pavlov's discovery can be used to train a human being ... Of course you can teach a child to read that way—nothing easier than that. You show him the word *chicken* seventeen times in succession, each time in connection with a picture of a chicken and an explanation by the teacher that this combination of letters means a chicken ... Don't you see how degrading the whole process is? The child is never told *why* this heap of letters means 'chicken'.

Obviously this method provides little technique for deciphering unfamiliar words. In some classrooms one can see a line of children waiting to be told 'what the word says'. In large classes, the use of this method does produce particular difficulties. Children are encouraged to recognize words by their shape or pattern, but also to think what particular word would fit into the context. I remember reading with a small boy who stuck on a three letter word beginning with *b*. The reading material was about a washing line of clothes with an appropriate illustration. Foolishly ignoring the picture 'clue' I said, 'Now you think what's on your Mum's line at home that begins with that letter.' A look of anticipated success passed across his face as he cried, 'Mum's bra.' The word in the text was *bib*.

Terms such as 'configuration', 'word-pattern', 'total form' and 'internal characteristics', tend to be used in books on this method rather than the word 'letters' and as Diack (1965) has pointed out 'the mental attitude of thinking about words as not being primarily composed of letters is reinforced'. Not looking closely enough at the letters in words can lead to individual letters being ignored and to guessing; e.g. *bra* for *bib*.

One would have supposed that not being confined by the restrictions of only using regularly phonic words (*mat, hop*, etc.), would lead to the production of more interesting *reading materials* firmly based on children's interests. However, if letter clues are underplayed, it does become difficult for the child to recognize easily the few hundred words necessary for the telling of an interesting story. For children to recognize even 'interest' words it is found necessary to *frequently repeat* them. Also if one has *fewer* words it is still easier. This has led to readers or primers with strict vocabulary control, which in practice tend to be few words frequently repeated. Beginning books in schemes have come to have less than 20 words, and Diack (1965) carrying the idea firmly to its logical conclusion has asked whether even these twenty words are necessary. 'From one point of view, no. The pictures tell what story there is and if reading is *at all stages* a matter of getting meaning from the printed page, then those twenty words are all of them unnecessary. So the wordless method had virtually arrived.'

Although there is insufficient space here to go into it in detail, the Gestalt theory of learning has been used as the theoretical basis for word methods, and basic ideas in this area of thinking are the importance of the *whole*, the innate organization of perception, and the insight or sudden understanding of personal experience. It was thought that young children could recognize the whole word *aeroplane* long before they knew its component

letters—that there was a tendency for individuals to perceive 'in wholes'. To a large extent this type of thinking
ignores the time element and the effects of previous learning. Indeed skilled readers and adults may part see a word
then read it whole. The process or operation of the skill
becomes so automatic it is difficult to reflect and realize
how the skill has developed. The method has a certain
element of imitation in it and to this extent, it can be
simply the adult forgetting the difficulties of childhood
saying, 'Do as I do, this is the way', and failing to provide
the child with the real key to reading, means of visual and
auditory analysis. Stressing reading for meaning is much
more closely linked with the *performance* of the skill
rather than its gradual growth and development.

Also, the emphasis in the word method upon the meaning
and importance of word forms at the expense of the recognition of the importance of letters, illustrates my impression of the way in which reading research has concentrated
on one factor of the reading process at a time. By noticing
one aspect of the relationship, it has been difficult to keep
in mind the rest of the situation, but if we pay attention
to word form and ignore letter form, we play a game of
black-and-white thinking. There need be no controversy
between the word and phonic methods. Both are just
different ways of looking at the reading process and trying
to isolate one factor at a time for closer attention.

Sentence method

The sentence method is an extension of the word method
in that it emphasizes the importance of comprehension but
uses the sentence instead of the word as the unit of meaning, and tends to attach less importance to letter-names or
sounds. Although it is difficult to define a sentence, the
method tends to make use of reading material from the
beginning which is characterized by a group of printed

words that make sense, not single words. As with the word methods, context is used as an aid to recognizing unfamiliar words, reading material is based on children's interests and spoken vocabulary, although the actual speech patterns of children are not necessarily utilized. It is hoped that the use of continuous prose leads to children reading more fluently and rapidly. Again there is behind this idea an adult insight into the level of performance. Because children read aloud in a manner unlike their level of speech competency, it does not necessarily follow that they fail to understand what they read.

Recent research by the writer (1969) suggests that some teachers place considerable importance on the attribute of *fluency* as a criterion of children's reading progress. However, recent studies have shown that fluency may be characteristic of a higher level of reading attainment, which can only be acquired after passing through certain subsidiary stages, characterized by stumbling and by re-reading; e.g. the work of MacKinnon (1959) and Clay (1966, 1969) already mentioned.

In learning to read, repetitions and stumbling are not so much serious errors as means by which the teacher can diagnose the particular child's stage of reading development, and for the child, the means of reinforcing correct responses. Word-by-word oral reading often in the past looked upon as a sign of poor oral expression—'barking at print'—may serve a very real function in the learning process.

Both word and sentence methods are important, emphasizing as they do the importance of obtaining meaning from what is read. But to the extent that they emphasize the function of the skill and the quality of its performance, they underrate the skill's complexity and the long and often slow process of acquiring it. Also, they ignore the importance of being able to use reading in a flexible manner; e.g. adapting the rate of reading to *what* is read.

40

Teachers often use both methods, sometimes starting with the word and proceeding to the sentence, sometimes in the reverse order. Flash cards and matching devices are often an important part of the procedure. The word 'flash' is usually applied to cards with a single word or sentence rapidly presented to children so they are discouraged from looking at the letters in words, or words in a sentence as an aid to recognition, but rather are encouraged to recognize 'at a single glance', a familiar word or a short easily understood and remembered phrase or sentence. Words or sentences may have distinct personal meaning for the children with whom the teacher uses this type of teaching apparatus. Teachers need to be aware of the way in which children are identifying and recognizing words; for instance, that they are not recognizing the card with *the* on it from the milk stain on the back of it rather than letter or word shape clues.

The use of matching devices may proceed through a series of development tasks, such as:

(a) matching two pictures of an object;

(b) observing the picture with its appropriate word label;

(c) matching separate word and picture cards;

(d) matching word and word—no pictorial clue, moving away from the *concrete* level;

(e) then the stages b—d may be repeated using a sentence or group of words in place of a single word label.

The 'language experience' approach

Some teachers, of course, realize that individual children or groups of children have different experiences and encourage them to share these with the class as a whole. Sometimes the experience is initiated by the teachers and children are led to talk about what they have been doing. The teacher and children write these oral expressions on the blackboard or in individual news books or class 'books'—often large sheets of stapled paper. Illustrations to accompany the children's words or phrases are added by the pupils. The children then read the material and become familiar with the words or phrases. Sometimes the teacher duplicates the sentences and phrases, and then these are matched starting with the whole sentence or phrase and proceeding to the individual words in the original 'news' or story in order to develop 'sight' vocabulary.

In this approach the emphasis is placed on experience as a basis for learning, and the reading materials are based on the child's own language. A popular variation is the practice of teachers encouraging children to draw pictures of their interests or 'News', the teacher then writing at the child's dictation the appropriate caption. It is intended that during the recording process the children will observe the relationship of speaking to writing and reading. Discussion about the captions leads to pupils learning about sound and symbol, the alphabet, repetition of words and symbols, punctuation, sentence meaning. Later the child writes his own reading material which the teacher may edit. At this stage he will need formalized spelling instruction and vocabulary development; he may be encouraged to make his own 'word file' or record new words in alphabetic order in a word dictionary of his own compiling. Eventually he uses more formal published materials.

Believers in this approach feel that one of the most important results is the concept the pupil develops about himself and about reading. Two American proponents (Lee and Allen, 1963) have outlined a sequence which they believe children follow as they learn by this approach:

1. What a child thinks about he can talk about
2. What he can talk about can be expressed in painting, writing, or some other form

3. Anything he writes can be read

4. He can read what he writes and what other people write

5. As he represents his speech sounds with symbols, he uses the same symbols (letters) over and over

6. Each letter in the alphabet stands for one or more sounds that he makes when he talks

7. Every word begins with a sound that he can write down

8. Most words have an ending sound

9. Many words have something in between

10 Some words are used over and over in our language and some words are not used very often

11. What he has to say and write is as important to him as what other people have written for him to read

12. Most of the words he uses are the same ones which are used by other people who write for him to read.

It should be noted that this approach includes at various stages emphasis upon sentences, words, letters and letter-sound correspondence. It proceeds from the egocentric stage of the child's cognitive development to growing interest in other people. To this extent, it is a balanced programme but it demands from the teacher some form of recording of individual children's vocabulary growth and diagnosis of their progress in phonic knowledge. It is not an easy approach to use in large classes. It has little in the way of training in visual and auditory ability built into it. It is very dependent upon children attaching importance to writing and reading as valid means of expression, in comparison say with painting, 'play' and other forms of free activity.

Individualized reading

Some of the more recent text books on teaching reading refer to 'individualized reading', particularly American ones, although other terms in the literature for similar types of approach seem to be 'free reading', 'personal reading', 'self-selected reading' or 'voluntary reading' (!).

Most teachers in this country encourage their pupils to 'read on their own' and the well-stocked reading or library corner is a recognition of children's need to browse and find their own level of reading matter. However, 'individualized reading' seems to be a decision by the teacher to give pupils guidance in reading on an individual basis, often because of a revulsion against a formal and rigid use of the familiar methods of teaching reading and particularly in regard to the 'thin gruel' of the published reading scheme and the unhappy division which can occur between reading 'primers' or readers and 'good children's literature'.

Some generally accepted characteristics of this approach are (a) a wide range of books placed strategically in various parts of the classroom on easily accessible shelves or racks; (b) the teacher keeps a record of each child's choice; (c) the children write a 'book report' or a short account of the book's contents, most interesting aspect, funniest incident, etc. in their own words (sometimes a list of interesting or difficult words is kept as well); (d) the teacher collects together in a small group for special instruction children who appear to have a common instructional need (e.g. work on beginning consonants; practice in phrasing; encouragement to work out more effective outlines; or advice on how to 'skim'). The focal point, however, is the teacher's individual conference with each child, the child reading both orally and silently, the teacher making notes of interests, instructional needs, general effectiveness on some sort of cumulative record sheet.

The writer's impression is that getting sufficient time within the daily programme for browsing, reading, and pupil-teacher conferences, as well as ensuring each child's instructional needs and also that their interests are satisfied, takes expert organization. Instruction cannot be erratic when it deals with a complex process such as reading and some attempt must be made to ensure that the more complex skills can be built upon the simpler ones. Certainly provision of adequate reading materials may be a task in itself and the teacher will need to regularly consult a range of publishers' catalogues, and the helpful publications on children's books which devote themselves to sorting out the wheat from the chaff; e.g.

(a) *The School Librarian* (published by the School Library Association) which contains useful articles and book reviews divided into sections, and written by specialists;

(b) *Growing Point* (published from Ashton Manor, Northants.) in which a very experienced connoisseur of children's books, Margery Fisher, writes on new and old books, with the accent on books which appeal to the middle-ability child; and

(c) *Children's Book News* (published from the Children's Book Centre, 140 Kensington Church Street, London W.8) which reviews children's books under classified sections.

Without careful help, children may choose books that because of their 'readability' level will not help them progress. Here I am thinking equally of the child who continually chooses a book that is at too low a level as of the child who tries a book too difficult to read—and what of the child who continually opts out? Teachers may need to do some sort of preliminary grading or assessing of book levels or be knowledgeable enough (and the school sufficiently well-endowed) for them to suggest alternative titles on particular subjects. Grading books is an extremely difficult task—length of sentence and number of syllables per word are some guide—but teachers may find some help with this matter by consulting the *First and Second Bristol Surveys of Books for Backward Readers* (University of London Press) published 1956 and 1962; *Help in Reading— Books for the Teacher of Backward Children and for Pupils*

Backward in Reading (National Book League); *Children's Reading* by K. S. Lawson (University of Leeds Institute of Education); *A List of Published Reading Schemes for the Primary School* by E. J. Goodacre.

Successful users of this approach list a number of advantages of the individualized approach, but the most important seem to be that the child proceeds under his own motive and drive, he reads at his own pace, interest is increased because he reads material of his own choice, each child is taught the skills that he needs when he needs them and so he realizes their usefulness, and the individual 'conference' promotes a close personal relationship between teacher and child.

4

Linguistics and the teaching of reading

It has already been mentioned that linguists have been critical of teachers' methods of teaching children the sounds of the letters and sound-letter relations. Also, in discussing the sentence method, I sometimes used the phrase 'a group of words' because an accurate definition of a sentence as a unit of meaning is not always easy. For instance, some modern linguists use the term 'phonological unit' (a measure of sound waves), which despite the number of the so-called sentences in it, or the interminable run-on nature, seems to be synonymous with a sentence as a unit of meaning. A phonological unit ends when the speaker shows by falling intonation or silence that he has reached a terminal point. In other words, a sentence in written language is connected with the convention of the use of a capital letter, a verb and a full stop. In spoken speech the 'sentence' is something else again. Indeed, a great deal of the present work being done by linguists is concerned with the effort to evolve a technique of analysis of the *internal structure* of both spoken and written speech.

Linguists may be critical of the reading teacher's ideas on language, its structural form and the teaching of 'sounds', but to many teachers of reading it seems that linguists underrate the complexity of the reading process. Certainly, many linguists subscribe to the belief that speech is the primary language function and that writing or reading are secondary or are even derived from oral language.

Importance of speech and language development

It is not surprising therefore to find current in their writings the ideas that (a) simple 'ordinary' speech development is all that a child needs to be ready for systematic reading instruction; (b) reading is very dependent upon auditory memories—being able to recall the sound patterns of speech; (c) comprehension or understanding of what he reads depends in the main upon the reader's ability to 'hear' or internally conjure up the sound of the written word in its normal inflection and to hear the combination of stress, tone and pitch of what is read to give it 'meaning'. At least one linguist has questioned these ideas by pointing out that children such as deaf-mutes can learn to read. The foreign-born, the bilingual and the hearing-impaired can learn to read and write, and these are all children whose auditory memories for spoken language are disadvantaged.

How far does speech coincide with written language? Does speech fulfil a superior function to reading? Harrell (1957) has produced evidence that the length of written stories does not correspond to oral compositions and that written stories tend to share more complicated sentences (as indicated by the index of subordinate clauses). Studies using a technique called 'transformational grammar' have indicated that oral compositions show significant differences from written language in structural elements at various age levels and therefore possibly different stages of children's cognitive development. (Spache, 1968, has described transformational grammar as a system of analysis 'which attempts to interpret the manipulation of syntactic units, as by expansion, reduction or rearrangement of basic or kernel utterances or by the combining of several sentences into one'.) Marquardt (1964) has noted also a number of differences between reading aloud and conversation, including the even tempo used in reading, the relationship of pauses to grammatical structure in oral reading as contrasted with the unpredictability of such pauses in conversation, the lack of meaningfully filled silences in oral reading in comparison with the frequency of these (accompanied by shrugs, grimaces and gestures) in conversation, and the repetitive structurally incomplete nature of conversation, particularly the use of almost meaningless phrases and words ('you know') to ensure rapport with the listener or provide the speaker with thinking time.

Obviously some of the difficulties between linguists and reading teachers result from the linguists' ideas about 'ordinary' speech and the development of language. Reading the writings of some linguists one has the impression that they underrate the effects of environmental factors (e.g. social class differences in speech usage, institutional effects on early language development of children). The more recent studies of children's writing and speech seem to concentrate on the analysis of syntax (i.e. sentence construction and rules of grammar, etc.) and although this is valuable, one needs to know more about the effects upon language development of family relationships and parental personalities.

In this country, Bernstein and his colleagues have studied the relationship between language and social factors. Bernstein has suggested that if the social relationship is close (i.e. much is shared in the speakers' environment) then a *restricted language code* can operate (heavy dependence on gesture and facial expression, short 'sentences', few logical connections used because it is assumed the listener is familiar with the content of the conversation). When the relationship is not close, more has to be put into the 'messages' (sentences are longer, more clauses used) and the speaker uses an *elaborated code*. According to Bernstein, the middle-class child is exposed at home to *both*

49

codes while the lower-class child's environment is that of the restricted code.

From work on readability measurement (Chall, 1958; Bormuth, 1964), it would seem that the restricted and elaborated codes of Bernstein are basically simpler or more complex forms of spoken language, and as applied to reading materials would be written language that is easier or harder to read. In this connection, the *cloze procedure* has provided us with information about how readers derive meaning of unknown words from the reading content. This technique involves the deletion of words from printed passages, the reader being expected to supply the exact word that has been left out. The deletions may be every fifth, tenth or whatever determined word, constituting what is termed a structural or 'any-word' deletion, or there may be selection of particular parts of speech (e.g. noun, verb)—a lexical deletion. The test may be given before or after reading the original text. Many of the studies using the technique use an 'every fifth word' deletion in a pre-cloze procedure, i.e. before reading the undeleted text. The cloze technique can serve not only to measure the reading difficulty of passages, but also as a measure in studies of learning, motivation and personality, and as a teaching device. It may be a valid means of studying the syntactic and semantic effects of context on language units and their basic differences.

Broadly speaking then, linguists have tended to minimize the differences between speech (restricted or elaborated) and reading (oral or silent) of reading materials (easier or harder to read).

Reading as 'decoding'

Three linguistic specialists, Bloomfield, Barnhart and Fries, have been taken fairly seriously in the last decade by those interested in the teaching of reading. They believed that the process of learning to read could be simplified if linguists could identify the basic speech sounds in English, and establish the relationships between these sounds and the letters that usually represented them. In the reading schemes they designed, the most frequent and most regular phoneme-grapheme correspondences were taught first. They also considered the best way to teach these correspondences in words carefully selected to permit the learner to discover for himself the relationship between letters and sounds. They disliked the isolation of sounds, and the teaching of 'phonic rules'. They were opposed to the use of pictures and to encouraging the learner to use context clues, since this might distract from the main task—paying close attention to the *letters*. Words used in practice reading material for the beginner were chosen on the basis of correspondence already taught, e.g. 'Nan had a fat cat' (Bloomfield); 'Dan can pat the cat' (Fries). Thus gradually the most common spelling patterns were mastered by reading orally words which contain these patterns. The learner avoided the irregularities of English which might confuse him and gained plenty of practice in applying the alphabetic principles or relating spelling to spoken language.

Levin's experiments (1966) suggest that this type of programming of one sound for one spelling pattern may have limitations (i.e. mastering *can, man, tan* and then moving to *cat, mat, rat*). Although Levin found that it takes longer to learn two sounds for one letter (e.g. to learn that *g* is pronounced as in *garage* and *giraffe*), than to learn one association at a time, dual association learning has a greater transfer value (e.g. more useful in a wider context). Thus systems that teach single associations may be easier for beginners, but their transfer value for 'real' reading is limited, since English spelling has not been reformed and more than one sound for one letter or letter groupings occurs.

Further, more recent analyses of English words by

linguists go considerably beyond the simpler correspondences put forward by Bloomfield (e.g. Venezky and Weir, 1966). Work by Chomsky and Halle (1968) suggests that there are more complex and powerful rules for the relations between spoken and written words and that English spelling may indeed make more sense than we have been led to believe by the purely descriptive linguists, since it supplies the native speaker with considerable syntactic and semantic information—'clues' and expectations in regard to both the meaning of particular words and the meaning of the total phrase or paragraph. As Chall (1969) has suggested, when analysed on a deeper level, retaining the 'silent' *g* in *sign* and silent *b* in *bomb* makes sense when we come to the derivatives *signal* and *bombardier*. Also Chomsky believes that written language has a life of its own— at a certain point it is not a direct representation of the spoken language, but a carrier of complex semantic and syntactic information.

Probably a 'decoding' type beginning programme may be useful but if children are kept on it too long—looking for graphic similarities—they are receiving insufficient practice in using syntactic and semantic cues, and therefore fail to develop flexibility in reading techniques. The danger is that children kept too long on a programme in which there is a consistent correspondence between letter and sound may become conditioned to this aspect of the reading situation, developing a 'mind set' for consistency which impedes progress.

Early training probably should emphasize building up a large bank of words and concepts, nouns and main verbs, so the child is able to deal with or process a *wide* variety of ideas. But at the same time, there should be ample exposure to varying structural patterns or writing styles to permit reactions to variations in sentences. Roberts (1969) has referred to the way in which the use of books of the rigidly controlled type tended to produce the same characteristics of language style in the written work of the children using them.

In case I appear to have been overcritical of the contribution of linguistics, let me hasten to add that linguistics has a great deal to offer the classroom teacher but I believe it is up to educators to apply this knowledge. Certainly some aspects which deserve consideration are the following:

Linguistics can provide the reading teacher with a fairly accurate description of the spoken language; techniques for language and reading research, e.g. cloze technique; new criteria for judging the readability of reading materials; new insights into children's language and how to describe more accurately the way children learn; and clues on how language conveys meaning.

Oral reading errors or 'miscues'

In a study of oral reading, Biemiller (1968) found a fairly regular progression in the types of reading aloud errors made by beginners. He divided these into three stages; the first being characterized by a preponderance of substitution errors showing heavy reliance on the context i.e. guessing. Some children remained at this stage a full year, most went on to a second, 'non-responding' stage, particularly the better readers—stopping to think and sub-vocally try out alternatives, consider letter or word 'clues', to be prompted or helped by the teacher; the third phase was characterized by greater flexibility in the strategies used to identify difficult words. Biemiller noted that all children seemed to go through these stages—the better readers at a faster rate; e.g. considering one thing at a time—context, letter clues, then learning how to deal with more than one factor and developing increasing mastery of this 'trial-and-error' technique.

Goodman (1969) has suggested that reading should be thought of as a 'psycholinguistic process' in which the reader, as a user of language, processes three kinds of information; 'grapho-phonic'—letter/sound clues, syntactic —grammatical constraints, and semantic—word meaning knowledge, as he reacts to the words on the page. Goodman outlined a method of comparing unexpected responses in oral reading to expected responses, which provides evidence of the nature of the reading process and how it functions. Studying children's oral reading errors can show the type of cues being used by the young reader, and the teacher can become aware of the strategies the child is using; e.g. correction—is the 'miscue' or error corrected; habitual association—strong associations which influence the reading, a *happy occasion* read as a *happy birthday*; dialect and syntactic differences—*we were* read *we was*; graphic proximity—*batter* read *butter*; phonemic proximity—*quietly* for *quickly* or distinguished by intonation *two* for *too*.

Christenson (1969) has looked at errors in relation to the type of reading matter and concluded that certain kinds of errors occurred more at the frustration level of reading. For instance, errors tended to be in the middle of words because the reader finding the material difficult used words which began or ended correctly but failed to use context and/or vowel sounds to check his efforts.

Teachers seem to be realizing that a child's imitation of the reading skill—achievement of an adult-type fluency— may not guarantee that he can use the skill effectively for his own purposes. By tolerating children's lack of fluency at a certain stage of their progress, listening attentively to their 'miscues', stumbling and repetitions, the teacher can learn much about the strategies being used by individual pupils. Also, valuable insights can be gained into the functioning of the reading process.

5
Development of visual perception

Research suggests young children do not perceive detail accurately. As they grow older, they are better able to analyse perceptual material and differentiate its parts. Eventually they are able to reorganize these percepts in such a way as to select and emphasize the *relevant* aspects of the situation and to ignore the rest. Of course, social conventions or the nature of the task tend to determine what is important and unimportant.

Work by Ames et al. (1953) has already been mentioned in which young children (two-year-olds) tended to perceive Rorschach inkblots as wholes, naming them as actually representing objects rather than being just vaguely like them in form. The older children, however, appeared to see more details and to attempt to interpret all of these, or to organize the material so as to include a number of the details. Later, Ames and Walker (1964) reported that the better readers were those children who had noted more details.

Learning what is significant

In the process of learning to read, children have to learn to attend to the detailed differences and similarities between *letter* shapes, and the forms and positioning of *words*. We know that by school age a great many children can see the small differences of detail involved in distinguishing one letter from another. Gibson et al. (1962) carried out an experiment in which children (four to eight) had to pick out 'letter-like shapes' from among others which differed only in certain details. Few mistakes were made in regard to differences between curved and straight lines and between continuous and broken lines (errors of closure). Rotations and reversals (errors involving shapes back to front or upside down) were more common among the younger children but decreased with age, possibly because position in space was learned to be significant in the perception of letters, i.e. the effect of their schooling. In a similar experiment with real letters, the same types of errors appeared but less frequently. In another Gibson study, it was found that the greater the number of similar details in letters, the greater was the tendency for the children (four-year-olds) to confuse them. Again, the ability to differentiate seemed to depend on the child's ability to see the difference between curved and straight lines.

It may be better to introduce the capital letters first since there is a greater difference in detail between these letters, e.g. A B C D, than the lower letters, *a b c d*. Certainly, before coming to school certain children notice for themselves the difference between capital letters used in street signs, car numbers and the words on cereal packets. Often these forms of the letters are large in size as well.

There has been some discussion between investigators as to whether the average child's eyesight is sufficiently mature for reading of small print, much before the period six to eight. Some researchers have suggested that the phenomenal success claimed for certain early beginning to read programmes may be attributable in part to the fact that a great deal of emphasis has been placed upon the use of film strips, charts, and other large-type materials to be read at some distance. In the use of large-size print, the relevant distinguishing characteristics of letters and words may stand out much more. Webster (1967) has suggested that a major contributory factor in difficulty with reading may be that 'children are forced to contend with what amounts to "whispered print", which decreases awareness of the essential characteristics of individual word shapes'.

Physical factors

Obviously a major physical factor in learning to read is the child's vision. Two aspects of vision are usually described in books in teaching reading:

(a) *visual acuity*—the child's ability to see at a distance and at near point or close-up—the quality and sharpness of what he perceives in his environment.

(b) *visual discrimination*—the child's ability to detect differences and similarities in size, shape and colour—his ability to differentiate between words and letters.

School medical examinations are likely to detect uncorrected defects in vision, but the teachers' own observations can be important. Continuous rubbing of the eyes, squinting, or other signs of discomfort or inattention in a child, may suggest to the teacher the advisability of the child having a thorough eye examination.

Visual discrimination

In this chapter, I wish to deal mainly with the question of visual discrimination, the process by which the child learns to perceive and pay attention to details in his visual environment. From an early age children can see in some form two-dimensional shapes but their experiences and training affect how these are perceived. The ability to distinguish the *sequential order* of shapes and to be aware of their *orientation* appears to develop slowly. That is, young children are very interested in the activities and movements of objects, and become concerned with their use and function, particularly the practical significance of objects to the child himself. Only gradually is the social significance or the usual importance attached to objects by those around the child, learned and appreciated by him.

Reichard et al. (1944) found that with a test of sorting objects into groups, children aged four to five tended to sort in an idiosyncratic manner into categories based upon incidental and non-essential likenesses which seemed more obvious to the individual child than to other people. Up to eight and nine, they sorted according to the function and use of objects and only after that by means of abstract generalization. This would be in line with Piaget's stages. Probably being able to group and classify objects and situations enables the child to produce a semblance of order in his existence, but at this stage the categories he uses may be his *own* invention and from an adult point of view, quite illogical and unsystematic. Again, children may attach too much importance to particular 'cues' and too little to a balanced representation of all the relevant features. This can be seen when children say they are 'writing' and produce wavy lines that scrawl hurriedly across the paper, in imitation of the grown-ups' 'joined-up' writing. Letters, even if known are lost in the resulting 'screed'.

Importance of language

Although names may be incorrectly given to objects (all animals in the farm book are 'cows'), there is evidence that the use of language is of considerable value to children in their being able to correctly identify objects. For instance, children aged three to five can recognize faces more correctly when they have learned to attach names to them than when they have merely been shown them. O'Connor and Hermelin (1961) found that imbeciles (mental age four to six) were better able to recognize pictures of real objects when the names of the objects were said aloud, than when the pictures were presented without warning. It seemed that the *naming* impressed the pictures on their minds. In this connection it would seem important that in emphasizing the difference between letters (capital or lower case) names of some sort should be given to the letters—either the letter name or its sound (probably the short sound of the vowels and the more usual sounds of the consonants). This seems a preferable alternative to the use of phrases such as 'the snake' letter which although intended to provide an image or pictorial clue for identification purposes, may act as a limiting factor when establishing sound/symbol correspondences.

I remember watching my eighteen-month-old son using a letter matching in-set tray belonging to his older sister. He rummaged through the plastic letters saying, 'Where's the hammer-thing?' This turned out to be the capital letter T. Even more puzzling to me, but not to him, was 'Where's the bee-byes gone?' This was eventually found. It was H, which I suddenly realized was (viewed from a particular angle) his cot, or as he called it then 'his bee-byes'. I had not told him the letter names and he was making associations based on his own experience, but this very personal meaning seemed to help him in his sorting of the letters.

Visual memory

In recognizing letters in reading, the child must do more than discriminate between letters of similar shape. He must be able to *perceive and remember* each letter pattern as a whole. Visual memory is thus involved in being able to identify letters and recognize words. In regard to recognition of words, a basic premise in many of our popular reading schemes is that if a word is repeated often enough it will be automatically recognized. Certainly some words may not be recognized because they have not been observed frequently enough, but there are many words which do not have to be repeated because for a particular child they are highly emotive words and therefore more easily remembered and recognized. Few children have difficulty in recognizing and remembering comparatively long words such as *icecream, aeroplane, television.*

Obviously, combinations of letter shapes in whole words are even more complex than single letters. How can children learn to recognize different words? In the early stages, words may be differentiated by their length—*hot* is short, *balloon* is long, and manuals to some of the reading schemes suggest differences in the configuration or shape of words (of the same length) should be stressed; *swim* and *safe* are the same length and start with the same letter, but their configurations are very different. However, recent research (Marchbanks and Levin, 1965) previously mentioned, suggests that children pay less attention to the overall shape of words than to the beginning and last *letters.* The white space before and after words helps not only to define the form of words but also to bring out the clarity of beginning and end letters in words.

Through experience which possibly includes training, children learn to look more closely at the 'middle' of words. They learn gradually the significance of the order of letters in words. Changing the position of letters changes the word meaning, e.g. *meat, mate.* In the same way, changing the position of certain letter forms changes the letters in the word and hence the word meaning; e.g. *map, mad* or *dear, bear.*

Orientation or spatial positioning

It has been found that young children (six to nine years) recognize correctly more often those words containing no ascending or descending letters. However, since some of the words used were very short syllables, shortness may have been a factor making for ease of recognition. It is interesting to consider this finding in relation to the research by Bender and others, on the reproduction of complex figures in which it was reported that horizontal direction of lines was often applied carefully whilst vertical and oblique direction was not accurately achieved until five plus and nine respectively. It seems likely that confusion over the direction or degree of direction is involved in the reversal of letters such as *b* and *d*; (e.g. vertical, but which direction?). Errors of inversion (*p* with *b*) involving vertical differentiation, ascending or descending have been reported to disappear at about mental age six, whereas reversals *b* and *d*—both ascending letters but directional difference— persisted until mental age seven plus.

A study by Popp (1964) into which letters were most easily confused by pre-readers, found that the letters *u*, *q*, *d*, *h*, *p*, *v*, *b*, *e*, *f*, *i*, and *k*, all presented difficulties. She concluded that the confusion between letters tended to arise from *reversals* and *rotation* of letter forms rather than from what she termed 'close and break transformations', (i.e. differences between curved and straight lines) plus some confusion related to the presence of similar or identical lines in pairs of letters. The letter pairs in which the most errors were made were *p* and *q* and *b* and *d*, closely followed by *b* and *q* and *d* and *p*. Other pairs were as follows: *b/p*; *h/u*; *i/l*; *k/y*; *t/u*; *c/e*; *d/h*; *h/n*; *h/y*; *j/k*; *n/v*.

It has been reported that reversible letters caused more confusion to children aged five to seven when they were *included in words* than when they were shown in isolation. Reversals such as *b* and *d* or *p* and *q* seemed to cause more trouble than the inversions such as *b* and *p* or *d* and *q* or *n* and *u*. Probably many children can distinguish between the forms of individual letters by six plus, but they need another year to grasp direction and to remember which of the reversible letter *shapes* correspond to which sound. As they gain more experience in hearing words and reading for meaning, the context helps them to decide whether it is *dad* or *bad*.

Sequential order

Learning which way up letters go, or whether the stroke goes to the left or right is not easy. A sense of direction has to be learned as does the convention that the letters in words are read from left to right.

Piaget and Inhelder (1948) reported that when very young children copied figures where one shape was contained within another, although each shape might be fairly accurately reproduced, their relationship to each other was not easily achieved. This tendency towards 'centration' or an inability to see the interrelatedness between objects seems to be present at Piaget's pre-operational stage, and that in the early stages (below six approximately) children are incapable of directing their attention in a systematic manner to parts of a complex shape. Their attention wanders in a random fashion.

A much earlier study by Teegarden (1933) drew attention to this lack of consistency in direction of movement, suggesting that comprehension of the left to right sequence involved in reading develops slowly. Indeed Piaget found that only about a quarter of his six-year-olds consistently scanned from left to right. Gottschalk et al. (1964) using a naming pictures task, had the observer watch to see how systematically the columns and rows of pictures were scanned. The use of a reading order, scanning left to right, increased with age (children three to six). The researchers suggested however the gradual change of perception from a hit-or-miss process to a more stable one did not appear to be entirely a function of specific training, and they believed further research was necessary to clarify the interaction of maturational limits and the effects of experience at this stage of perceptual organization.

Research by Elkind and Weiss (1967) has shown that the way in which the perceptual material is itself organized, is likely to have an effect on the individual subject's perception at a certain stage in their cognitive development. The children (five to eight) in the study were asked to name structured and unstructured arrays of familiar pictures (in the structured array, the pictures were set out in a triangular pattern). Generally it was the six-year-olds who used a left-to-right pattern of scanning and the older children more complex combinations of patterns. The researchers related the patterning used to experience in reading and to Piaget's theory of cognitive stages. It appeared that perceptual development consisted in the gradual liberation of perception from the constraints of the physical properties of the array's configuration (e.g. the form of a triangle) to more adventurous patterns of scanning. It was noticeable that the left-to-right pattern persisted in the poor readers. In other words, they seemed to be less flexible in adopting a form of scanning appropriate to *this* particular task and utilized a habituated one. This practice in itself would condition them to continue this particular form of scanning.

In a number of experiments, Piaget has shown that children slowly acquire the concept of seriation—that is, they are able to order by size or reproduce the sequence of a pattern. The reader may recall Piaget's experiments in which the child has to reproduce a given order of beads on a string and at a certain stage, the child tends to see not the complete string but rather to perceive the proximity of each bead to the one before and after. Possibly a similar stage occurs in perception of letters in words. The child sees each letter within the word shape in relation to the preceding (scanning may be left to right or the reverse) rather than sequences or groupings of letters. However with increasing experience of print, he develops expectations regarding the probable occurrence of particular letter sequences or letter strings in words. Thus, once one or possibly two letters are seen, the remainder of the word or the particular syllable is anticipated (e.g. *q* always followed by *u*—also writing helps imprint the correct orientation of the letter *q*). An important factor at this stage, is the effect of writing practice which forces the child not only to attend to *letter shapes* but also to the exact order or *letter sequence* within words.

Transfer of training

It is interesting to note that the ability to string beads has been found to be a fair predictor of reading (Orpet et al., 1966). Does this mean children must have grasped the concept of seriation in order to be able to progress in reading? For instance, training in the capacity to perceive shapes other than letters does not seem to increase reading ability. Goins (1958) trained six-year-old beginners for a term in perceiving and recording geometrical shapes and digits shown briefly. Although their performance at this task improved, they were no better at reading than children who did not receive this particular type of training. This raises the whole question of *transfer of training* (e.g. the effect which some particular course of training has on learning or carrying out a second performance). The effect may be helpful (positive) or it may interfere and make it more difficult (negative). Research on this problem suggests that what is important is how the learner goes about the initial task and consciously makes generalizations about what he is doing. Methods or techniques used in the initial task are more likely to be transferred when the learner becomes clearly conscious of their nature and their general applicability. Probably transfer effects are limited and what is transferred is either very specific elements (applicability depending on the similarity of the tasks) or broader principles, methods, ideals and attitudes—that is, *how* to tackle the task. But such broader transfer does not usually take place unless the learner has his attention drawn to these points and he becomes aware of their value and their applicability.

Intelligence seems to be one of the main factors in transfer, for the more intelligent the child, the more likely he is to *realize for himself* the possibilities of transfer. Also, individuals vary in their ability to 'catch on' to features of different complexity—to see what are the common features of different complexity—to see what are the common features between stringing beads and scanning the letters in words from left to right.

Also, sociologists have suggested that different ways of attacking learning problems are related to social class factors. The 'culture' of the working-class is such that children from this type of social background are more likely to avoid and fear the 'unusual', viewing it as a threat to their habitual way of thinking. By comparison, the middle-class child is encouraged to be more curious and to look for common features in different learning situations, thus extracting learning principles from his varied experiences.

Visual perceptual abilities

Various researchers have observed that several visual perceptual abilities are involved in the process of recognition and discrimination, and a test of visual perception—*The Marianne Frostig Developmental Test of Visual Perception* (1964)—has been devised to isolate and evaluate five of these abilities. The sub-tests in the battery of tests are said to be a measure of:

(a) *eye-hand co-ordination*: the child has to draw lines between guide lines or toward a target.

(b) *figure-ground perception*: the child is asked to trace intersecting figures and overlapping figures without being confused by intervening lines. This sub-test evaluates the ability to see certain parts of the visual field as distinct from background features—to be able to see the trees and not be distracted by the wood. This seems to be similar to Piaget's idea of 'decentration'.

(c) *form constancy*: the child has to outline only squares or circles on pages containing other shapes. This is to evaluate the ability to recognize *shapes*, regardless of their patterning, colour, size, background or position in space. This is probably the ability which is related to whether a child can easily see the difference between *n* and *h*; *hay* and *bay*.

(d) *position in space*: the child needs to differentiate between a specific figure and identical figures, which are reversed or rotated. This is to evaluate the child's ability to perceive the direction of an object in relation to himself. Children weak in this area have difficulty with reversals of letters and words long after other children have got them sorted out.

(e) *spatial relationships*: the child copies a figure by drawing lines between dots. This is to see whether the child can perceive points or shapes in relation to each other as well as in relation to himself. Children writing *h s i s p* or *ships*—scrambling words—may have difficulties in this area. Letter sequences are not easily learned.

The various difficulties in reading that occur as a result of disabilities in each of these various areas are discussed in Chapter 7.

Perception and personality

The ability to analyse the perceptual situation actively and to differentiate its parts seems to some extent to be related to important personality differences which may or may not be related to social class factors. Witkin et al. (1962) showed that differences existed with children over eight, and they formulated the term 'field independence'. It seems that some children are able to treat their physical environment fairly objectively, and to understand its basic nature, and use this comprehension for satisfying their own needs, whereas other children are more influenced by the environment generally and easily distracted from their analytical pursuits. This separateness from the environment may have a constitutional basis but it also seems to be influenced by the mother's personality and how she has encouraged her child to tackle learning situations.

A number of researchers have looked at this question of learning styles. Field dependence-independence seems to be used to describe the ability to abstract an item from the field in which it is embedded—to see it in its own right as it were. The work of Kagan (1965) is relevant at this point. He has postulated two stable dimensions upon which both children and adults seem to be distributed. The first is called *reflection-impulsivity*—the degree to which a child can consider alternative classifications or solutions, or must 'jump to a conclusion'. The reflective type of child or adult seems to characteristically delay decision taking until the alternatives available have been enumerated and their validity assessed. This type of individual behaves as if he cared that this first response or action is as correct as possible. Kagan has described a second dimension called *visual analysis* which appears to be a tendency to analyse complex stimuli into their component parts; that is, some children are able to break down the stimulus into small subunits whereas others label and react to a larger 'chunk' of material. Kagan considers these two dimensions to be independent of each other.

Another experiment by Kagan and his associates (school

beginners analysing complex shapes and extracting elements from whole patterns) showed that some children were consistently deliberate and reflective, and inhibited impulsive action. The reflective children a year later were those who were the more accurate in word and letter recognition.

Personality and types of reading material

Obviously cognitive styles must play some part in the way in which the reader understands and interprets what he sees, which includes what he or she reads. Probably in some types of reading the individual already has many concepts and the reading of this material is a comparatively simple task of recognition and association. In another type of reading, the child may have only a limited number of concepts which apply and so make only a few associations, probably involving considerable effort. In a third type of reading, the reader may have little or no familiarity with the information being received, and therefore must rely mainly upon the actual information in the words themselves.

Deighton (1959) has pointed out that what the context reveals to a given reader is dependent upon his background of experience. Context can reveal meaning through definitions, examples, restatements and inference. Deighton felt inference provided about half the meanings used, and inference would of course be related not only to the child's background but also to Kagan's dimension of reflection—impulsivity. Cognitive style must play an important part in the degree of persistence the reader brings to the task.

However, some evidence suggests that the teacher can directly influence children to read more critically. Research on teacher-pupil classroom interaction has shown that the teacher's own verbal behaviour influences children's level of thinking as well as their attitudes and achievement. A crucial ingredient in improving the effectiveness of the teacher's influence, is the teachers' own accurate perception of what they are doing in the classroom. Teachers need to realize that they do have direct control over the *types* of questions that are discussed with pupils (e.g. not always the recall of factual information type of answer), the quantity and quality of children's participation in discussion, and the stimulation of levels of thinking employed (e.g. concrete, abstract).

Wolf (1967) and his associates found that children throughout their schooling could be taught to read critically, the teachers' questions influencing the depth of their thinking. The primary school teachers tended to ask more questions requiring a recall of specific facts than questions which required pupils to evaluate, analyse or frame hypotheses. Other researchers have found that quite young children have the ability to do some critical thinking, but again it was the teachers' type of questions which influenced the depth of thinking. Wolf, although finding intelligence positively related to critical reading, found the effects of instruction were the same for each intelligence level. He concluded therefore that all children could benefit from the sort of teaching which encouraged 'critical reading'.

However, both teachers' questioning and children's interpretations will be related to their individual attitudes, values and beliefs. Some researchers have analysed the feelings of bias, prejudice and religious belief that are likely to affect one's attitudes to social, moral and ethical problems encountered in one's reading. Both children and their teachers need to be able to *differentiate* between their own emotions and attitudes, and those which are expressed by the writer in reading materials of an emotive nature. This, of course, needs to be extended to an understanding of the devices of propaganda and an analysis of their function and influence.

69

It is of interest, I think, that Wolf found the relationship between critical reading ability and personality factors to be low, but the correlation for the secondary age group to be slightly higher than for the younger group. Children emerge from the egocentric stage, and other people's views and opinions assume importance. It is then that styles of cognitive behaviour (e.g. 'jumping to conclusions', inability to play with ideas, dependence on group opinions) become habitual forms of reaction.

6
Development of auditory perception

In learning to read, not only must the child be able to discriminate and recognize letters and words, but to make any real progress he must be able to learn the sounds of letters and words and associate them with their visually perceived shapes. In the last chapter, I differentiated between visual acuity and visual discrimination. In the same way with auditory discrimination one needs to distinguish between different aspects of the hearing process. A common assumption is that once the ability to hear has appeared, it is wholly functional and ready to work as soon as it makes its appearance. It is too often believed that once a child is able to hear, he is able to understand the spoken word; that when he can understand the spoken word, he can distinguish each sound within the word; that when he can distinguish each sound, he can monitor or correct his own speech or can use this knowledge of phonetics to attack new words by 'sounding them out'.

This would be a logical sequence of events, but all the research points to audition or hearing as a function in which various aspects develop at different rates and do not work together easily at all times. Audition seems to develop sequentially on at least three levels and there is a sequence of development at each level.

Learning to hear

One can distinguish at the initial level what is generally termed *acuity*. Wepman's (1960) definition is a useful one. He describes it as 'the ability of the ear to collect sounds from the environment and transmit them to the nervous system'. When these sounds reach the brain, they are interpreted only as sounds, noises, etc. unless previous experience has accumulated giving them meaning. As a mother of young children, I can give plenty of examples of the stage of understanding or interpreting sounds. A rhythmic series of thumps I can interpret as Teddy being dragged down the stairs, whilst an ear-splitting metallic crash is the tin of Matchbox toy cars being emptied on the playroom floor as a preliminary to playing 'garages' and 'car parks'. As many mothers know from experience, even silence can be interpreted, usually as a danger signal and the need to go and see 'what they are up to now'.

My children may have excellent auditory acuity but because of their background, French or Japanese will be a meaningless babble to them. Similarly, because of my inexperience, much of the 'Top of the Pops' programme on television comes to me as so much 'noise'

This ability to make sense of what one hears is of great importance to children in regard to their language development. By associating the continuous sound patterns which constitute speech as the meaningful words of language, children develop listening comprehension, or what some of the reading textbooks refer to as 'auding' ability. A further level of audition can be described. It involves *auditory discrimination and retention*. This is the ability of the child not only to differentiate each sound of his language from every other sound, but to hold each in mind well and long enough for him to moderate his speech or make accurate comparisons between the sounds he distinguishes and their representations in the printed language. Thus children learn to apply their hearing. The specific learning task is to distinguish sounds (phonemes) related to their written representation (graphemes).

Some reading experts also distinguish between *gross* and *fine* discrimination. The former is the ability to hear sounds which are quite unlike each other, whereas fine discrimination is the skill in distinguishing between sounds which are very similar. Gross discrimination is necessary for auditory comprehension, for understanding words in sentences, but fine discrimination is essential to hear grapheme differences within those words. For example, gross discrimination is involved in asking children questions such as 'Which shall I wear—a hat or a mat?' 'Which shall I play with—a ball or a beach?' 'Which makes a noise—butter or buzzer?' Finer discrimination would be involved in 'Was the ship wrecked on a wreath or a reef?' It has been suggested by workers in reading clinics that certain children do not develop the ability to make these fine aural distinctions until they are eight or nine.

Development of auditory abilities

Auditory acuity appears to develop in a set sequence; children responding first to the middle, then the low and finally the upper frequencies of tone. Auditory comprehension increases gradually, preceding speech. The very young child responds first to a few words using visual clues, intonation and gestures all as 'clues'. Gradually response is made to more words and to different combinations of words. Brown and Bellugi (1964) reported that young children selected the nouns and verbs more often than the adjectives from sentences heard. These are the high information words which receive the heavier stress in adult intonational speech patterns. For example, from the sentence 'Here comes Daddy in his car', the young child selects 'Daddy coming car', or even 'Daddy car'. The forms he leaves out

73

tend to be the grammatical functions or the low-information words; inflections, auxiliary verbs, articles, prepositions and conjunctions. These function words have meaning but it is meaning which comes gradually from content.

Oral vocabulary

Slowly, through imitation of the language patterns of the adults around him, older siblings, etc., the young child expands his oral vocabulary and learns to include these function words in his sayings. Suggested quantitative values for listening vocabularies by school age have been a median size of 14,400 words (Templin, 1957). However, more recent studies suggest that television is having an increasing effect on children's listening vocabularies, and that with the stimulation of television and other influences missing from the lives of their grandparents, many of to-day's children have listening and speaking abilities which range far beyond the type of language used in most introductory books of schemes.

To assume though that just because a child uses words and grammatical constructions 'correctly' he has a commensurate understanding of them would be a mistake. Piaget has provided many insights into how children can use grammatical forms before they can grasp the structure of meaning corresponding to them. That is, the use of language structure by a child is not necessarily a guarantee that the child has the understanding some adults would attribute to him.

Auditory discrimination

Auditory discrimination appears to follow a pattern similar to that of acuity. Discrimination of the high-frequency sounds appears somewhat later than those of the middle frequencies. Research on the development of speech in children points to the progressive nature of the acquisition of correct articulation. Work by Poole (1934) is often quoted which shows the *latest age* at which consonant sounds appear in normal children's speech.

'Age 3½ sounds mastered b–p–m–w–h
4½ „   „   d–t–n–g–k–ng–y
5½ „   „   f
6½ „   „   v–th (as in then)–sh–zh–l
7½ „   „   s–z–r–th (thin)–wh–ch–(j)'

What is important to note is that the sound acquisition in children's speech is progressive and that amongst normal children the particular speech sounds may not be correctly used until as late as seven or eight.

With these findings in mind, it is not surprising to recall that in Bruce's study (1964) of children's ability at auditory analysis, the children below mental age seven found the task very difficult and the successful amongst the older children were more likely to be those who had received some phonic teaching. The main difficulty seems to be that a spoken word is a continuous whole, and young children have had to learn to distinguish patterns of sound as the names of objects, actions, etc. It may be necessary to show them how to break up these slowly established units of meaning, for them to be able to hear in spoken words the sounds of the constituent individual letters and letter strings.

Distinguishing individual sounds

From speech errors, we can infer that for school beginners there will be certain sounds in speech which they have not mastered as yet. They will be unable to hear them accurately, and they fail to produce them correctly in their accepted positions in words. For instance, Stephen calls himself Teven. As the beginning s of his name is one of the sounds not mastered until the stage of infant schooling, it is probably because he does not hear the *s* part of the consonant blend *st* very accurately at his present stage of auditory development.

A distinction is sometimes made between *voiced* and *voiceless* consonants. The consonants *p—t—k—s—f* are voiceless consonants whose speech sounds are in the higher frequencies. The unvoiced digraphs *sh—ch—th* (as in *thin*) have this same distinguishing characteristic. Olmstead (1966) predicted in his theory of children's learning of speech sounds, that a voiced sound (the vocal chords vibrate during the production of the sound) would be easier to distinguish than a voiceless one. Some teachers of beginners check whether their children can hear these differences in sound involving pitch by asking them individually about orally spoken word pairs, e.g. *fin—fin; thin—bin;* am I saying the same thing or different words?

The *Wepman Auditory Discrimination Test* is based on this idea of using pairs of carefully selected words read aloud and therefore does not demand visual, speech or reading ability on the part of the child tested. The words used are ones familiar to young children and are all the same length. Comparisons are made of sounds in the same position in each word pair and each comparison is within the same phonetic category. For example, a word pair such as *cat—cap* is used to test the discrimination of final sounds. The test also includes a series of word pairs which are not different; e.g. *man—man.*

Another aspect of auditory perception that appears to be significant for reading is the ability mentally to fuse, blend or synthesize the sounds of word parts into whole words. Chall (1963) has reported evidence that a simple test of auditory blending correlated significantly with both oral and silent reading. In interpreting the findings, Chall has suggested that poor blending might be a symptom of neuro-physiological defect or a lag in development. An inability to blend sounds due to immaturity or to some sort of brain damage would, of course, be important when children try to attack unknown words.

Distinguishing a succession of sounds in familiar words

Similarly, it is a problem when children cannot distinguish the separate sounds within a word when they hear them as a sequence of sounds. In tasks involving the forming of concepts about objects, children are free to touch, see, smell, taste, and listen to them. They learn about the object's properties at a concrete level before proceeding to the stage at which they can think about the object without experiencing its presence. Speech is the means by which children can think about and talk about the absent object. The process of internalizing actions proceeds very gradually from the concrete (using the evidence of the senses) to the abstract.

How can one carry out this procedure when the objects in question are sounds? Children cannot see, touch, smell or taste sounds as such. They can only listen to them, and they are transitory, soon gone—unlike the written word which can be studied. Elkonin (1963) has suggested one way of making sounds materialize. Underneath the picture of an object, the teacher draws a box made up of horizontal squares, one square for each sound in the illustrated word. The name of the object is said, and as each sound in the word is spoken, a counter is placed in each square under the illustration. Then the word is said—as a whole—once more. In this way, the child starts from the concrete level (illustration of a familiar word) with the procedure being word as a whole, break down into constituent parts, word as a whole again. Gradually the child can be encouraged to carry out the procedure of sounding the parts and saying the whole for himself. The visual presentation and the handling of the counters provides a concrete level of operation for the abstract process of phonetic analysis. Eventually both pictures and counters should be withdrawn, so that the procedure is accomplished on the plane of audible speech.

Similarly, some teachers show children how to make the sounds of individual letters, letting them see for themselves in mirrors how their mouths form the sounds or encouraging them to feel their vocal chords as they sound the voiced consonants. Others encourage fun with sounds, giving them characters and personalities such as the 'flat tyre' sound of s— or the quiet sound of sh—, or asking children to listen to the sneeze sound in *chair, children* and *chocolate*. Post boxes can be made labelled *sh* or *ch* and children encouraged to post words beginning with the sound. In this country the old game 'I Spy' seems to be the favourite way of encouraging children to listen to beginning sounds, but many bright children get great enjoyment out of alliteration, trying tongue twisters and playing 'I went shopping for *butter, balls, banjoes*', etc. As soon as children are adept at these earlier, concrete levels, it is perhaps as well to ask them to verbalize the difference and say where words are different—beginning, middle or end—and relate these differences to graphic differences (how the word is written).

Some readiness books suggest a gross kind of discrimination such as hearing the difference between the dropping of a pin and the hammering of a hammer, but as with visual discrimination exercises, the most valuable training seems to be that involved in discriminating actual *speech* sounds, and discovering with which sounds children have difficulty.

Acquisition of phonic skills

Sims and Williams (1969) have carried out an interesting study of reading development based on a test of phonic skills which used 76 phonic elements. Each phonic element was embedded in a nonsense word. The child's phonic skill was assessed on the basis of his ability to recognize and pronounce (individual administration) or select and ring (group procedure) the nonsense word. The test covered short and long vowel sounds, initial consonant blends (e.g. *pl*; *br*) final consonant blends (*rm*; *rn*); vowel—vowel combinations (*ea*; *ai*; *ou*; etc.) consonant digraphs (final position—*ch*; *sh*; *th*) and special cases (*ble*; *tion*; *ight*).

Using scores on a group word recognition test, they found that little progress was made in associating phonemes and graphemes until a *reading* age of 6 years 8 months—7 years 2 months had been reached, and that a reading age range of 7 years 3 months—7 years 9 months was necessary before the progress became well established. They reported an interesting correspondence between the frequency of phonemes in adult speech, the spelling frequency of these sounds, and the difficulty level of these same 'phonic' elements as revealed by the test they used. It appeared that in reading, as in language development generally, children began with coarse or simple distinctions and progressed step by step to finer discriminations. The less frequent phonic elements were those least accurately discriminated. The researchers believed it was possible to distinguish developmental stages in pupils' ability to discriminate the graphic symbols for more frequently represented phonemes. The children discriminated short vowels and began to discriminate initial consonant blends between the reading ages of 6 years 8 months—7 years 2 months. At this stage few final consonants were accurately perceived. By 7 years 3 months—7 years 9 months reading age level, the majority of initial and final consonant blends were being recognized, whereas difficulties existed in regard to a long vowel in a word formed from a consonant blend, vowel, single consonant and final silent *e*, and of vowel—vowel combinations. Digraphs (*wh*; *th*; *ch*; *sh*) appeared to be learned at a later stage and mainly as part of 'spelling patterns in reading'. Unfortunately the sample was not big enough to look at differences in regard to differences in type of reading instruction the children had received. Also, meeting these phonic elements in meaningful words would have influenced the children's ability to decipher them.

Dialect and language patterns

A difficult problem is the effect of *dialect* differences. Labov (1967), who studied in detail the speech of Harlem negroes, found evidence of how the sound *d* is substituted for *th*, so that these children learn to read *dem* for *them* and *dey* for *they*. Even more difficulties occur in the pronunciation of vowels and end sounds. One study found that of the 220 words in Dolch's list of basic words in the English language, Negro dialect of this type changed 158.

Disadvantaged children in a New Orleans study when asked 'if a car ran over your pet, how would you feel?' answered 'good'. It seems such children tend to miss the hypothesis behind questions such as this, since they 'tune in' to key words only and rearrange these words in questions which make sense to *them*. They probably caught the words '... how ... you feel?' 'Good' was therefore a logical answer. They understood the meaning of each word, but did not understand the syntactical structure. They picked up the three key words and reframed them into the more familiar pattern 'How you feel?' Similarly, asked 'if you could be a policeman or a fireman, what would you choose?' the stock answer was 'gum'. Again the hypothesis of the question created problems for these children, complicated by the double meaning of the sound *chooz* (to *choose* something or to *chew* it). *Chews* was more familiar, so the question became 'What ... you chews?' In that context, *gum* made admirable sense.

The beginning method

The research outlined in Chapter 2 demonstrated that there is more than one method of presenting systematic instruction in reading. In our reception classes and at the beginning of infant schooling, however, initial reading instruction is more often than not restricted to visual presentation. For most children, this approach is effective. However, there are some children who need much preparation through the other senses before they are able to discriminate among letters and words with the necessary precision to assure effective sight recognition. The teacher needs to know something about the stages in perceptual development or she may make incorrect assumptions about the ability of particular children to learn by a single approach or method.

Some children make good progress initially and then seem to fall behind. They may have good memories but eventually the vocabulary load becomes too great for them to deal with it visually, and their memory for new words reaches its limit. Then, their inability to discriminate among sounds or their lack of success in acquiring phonic skills acts as a barrier for attaining the independent stage of reading. With these children, who have progressed but find they can no longer use the method they initially found successful, learning to handle failure may be the real difficulty. Their security has been shaken and they can far too easily become the problem backward reader.

In this and the previous chapter I have concentrated upon describing the development of visual and auditory abilities in children because these are basic to the reading process and to achieve progress children must learn to combine the two modes of thought. Referring to the research available, it is evident that the perceptual skills are slowly acquired, children gradually increasing their capacity to acquire more complex abilities with age.

7

Needs of individual children

In a book of this length, it is impossible to describe in great detail the symptoms of children's reading disabilities and the appropriate treatment for such defects. However, in the light of the discussion in the previous chapters of children's perceptual and cognitive development, it should be pointed out that children's rates of development vary greatly and in individual children development appears to be an uneven procedure. Either because of genetic differences or early brain damage, some children will evidence particular difficulty in coping with particular aspects of the developmental process. Other children, because of specific environmental conditions, will demonstrate faster or slower rates of adaptation to the school learning environment. In this last chapter, I want to describe certain categories of children, trying to pin-point what may be their particular needs in the classroom, and making suggestions as to how the teacher may identify their particular problem. Also, I have described approaches or materials which might prove useful.

Visually handicapped

The National Child Development study (1958 Cohort) figures (Pringle et al., 1966) suggest it would be a wise precaution for teachers to consider any child wearing glasses in a primary school as having defective vision and to place that child in preferential seating according to the eye condition. However, the above study also reported that over 13 per cent of the children examined who did not wear glasses had at least one eye with visual acuity below the optimum, taking 6/6 as perfect vision. Therefore it would seem advisable for teachers to be on the look-out for such behaviour patterns as the following, which may suggest that the child has difficulties of vision—rubbing eyes; excessive frowning; irritability when doing close work or reading; stumbling over small objects; holding books close to eyes; having red-rimmed or swollen eyelids; complaining about headaches or nausea following close eye work; having blurred or double vision. Sometimes an uncorrected visual defect manifests itself in restlessness, lack of interest in games or reading, or other activities requiring prolonged close use of the eyes.

The main eye defects are *squint* (strabismus) in which one eye is so weak it fails to move with the other; *short sightedness* (myopia) and *long sightedness* (hypermetropia) —defects usually compensated by the use of glasses with special lenses; *astigmatism* caused by uneven curvature of the lense of the eye which produces distorted images. A study by Shubert and Walton (1968) of the effects of induced astigmatism in college students, reported that confusion of similar letters and words in reading may be the result of visual blur and distortion produced by uncorrected astigmatism.

Of course, reading materials for *all* children should be carefully selected considering such things as clarity of type and pictures; spacing between lines, words and letters; quality of paper (e.g. whether it has a non-glossy surface); contrast between background and printing. But many partially-seeing children probably benefit from larger-than-

average print (18-point or 24-point).

83

Correspondence with the headmaster of a school for the partially-sighted elicited the information that his staff were careful to select well-printed books and in regard to a reading scheme considered the reading merits as much as the question of print size. Their programme was based on the *Queensway Scheme* (Evans) supplemented by books such as those in the *Reading with Rhythm* series (Longmans). Books in large print are beginning to be more numerous in this country although there is no reading scheme as such. These large print books are mainly reference books and general reading suitable for older children and the quality of print and content can be variable. F. A. Thorpe (Publishing Ltd), Artisan House, The Bridge, Anstey, Leicester, produce a list of the titles in the *Ulverscroft Series of Large Print Books* suitable for school libraries (includes a dictionary). The National Book League publication *Help in Reading* suggests the *Bart Books 1 and 2* (Birmingham Association of Remedial Teachers), *Looking at Words* (Hart-Davis) and *Terry the 'Tec*, as suitable material for the partially-sighted child. As can be seen, the range of books is somewhat limited.

In the chapter on visual discrimination, I described the visual perceptual handicaps and difficulties in spatial orientation diagnosed by using the *Frostig Developmental Test of Visual Perception*. Deficiencies in these abilities may reveal themselves in a child's difficulty in distinguishing left from right, in finding his place on the page, in reversal errors, in difficulty in copying accurately, in recognizing familiar sight words, or failing to remember the sequence of letters within words. In the classroom such children may be inattentive, easily distracted and clumsy, and in games show poor visual-motor co-ordination, e.g. eye and hand co-ordination.

Children with poor figure-ground perception may have difficulty in focusing on the printed page. A typical remark of such a child is that when asked whether or not he needed to point to words while he read, he replied firmly, 'Yes, if I don't hold the words down with my finger, they move all over the page.' Such children benefit from the use of an L-shaped marker which allows only the next word to be read to be seen, or even a 'window' type marker permitting only one word at a time to be exposed. Practice in finding certain words, letters, or answers in a page, or in crossing out letters while following a line of print, may be useful exercises. Children who have difficulty in doing the 'find the three hidden balls' type of picture on the front page of such young children's comics as *Teddy Bear*, may be experiencing figure-ground difficulties. They can benefit from tracing over each word (using different coloured crayons) in a page of words where the words are placed at different angles, often crossing one another.

Form constancy difficulties can be revealed in confusions between similarly shaped letters, e.g. *h, r, n*. (N.B. Children with uncorrected astigmatism may show the same difficulty, which emphasizes the importance of vision defects being ruled out *before* perceptual training is instigated.) Words of similar configuration may appear the same. Tracing round letter shapes, making letter shapes from circles and stick shapes of paper, copying words using felt cut-out letters, may help to draw the child's attention to the fine visual difference between letters and different words. Such children may benefit also from matching exercises involving the same word produced in different print styles, colour or size.

Children with poor ability in recognizing *position in space* often show it through letter and word reversals which persist after the infant stage of schooling. They may experience difficulty in reading the time on the clock or setting a table, or they may appear unaware of their own occupation of space and leave legs and arms about, or bump fingers, knees, etc. going through door spaces, yet apart from this seem of normal intelligence. Awareness of their own body can be developed by letting them assemble a figure from its parts (cut out of card or felt), or practice with the gross discrimination type of item found in reading readiness material, where children have to match a particular shape from a choice of shapes including reversals (mirror images) and upside down figures. For these children, it is probably very important to have correct examples of letter and numeral formation permanently on display in the classroom. Writing books with ruled lines may be necessary to help them realize the correct orientation of letters.

Handicaps in *spatial relationships* (spatial constancy) may show up in an inability to copy a model in stringing beads or copying dot patterns. Again, the way in which a child completes an exercise in bead stringing will show to what extent he is able to copy the whole pattern (correct colour and order) or is matching on a one-to-one basis. This handicap is probably closely related to cognitive development generally, and the teacher should in particular watch out for signs of poor visual imagery—difficulty not so much in copying patterns as reproducing series or patterns no longer seen. Training in visualization may be fostered by the teacher describing objects which have to be named, presenting stories orally which the child illustrates, or getting children to assemble objects or build constructions without visual or pictorial instructions. Games such as *Memory* (turning up and matching pairs of cards) or 'I went shopping and bought ...' (lists of objects orally remembered) can also benefit these children.

Many teachers use as their initial teaching method an approach which emphasizes visual presentation (e.g. look-and-say and sentence methods). For some children the configurations of words simply do not remain stable. The visual images of words vary and they have no other skills to aid their visual memory. Their problem is their inability to remember words by their shape. Their difficulty in mastering a sight vocabulary (however small) through a visual method causes them to lag behind their class mates and they are labelled as poor readers very early. This is a different situation to the child who learns quickly by visual methods but who begins to fail once phonics are introduced, because of poor auditory ability. With children who have done well and who suddenly discover in the top infants or first year juniors that the method they have been using no longer works (vocabulary load is too great to be dealt with solely by visual means), learning to handle failure may be the greater problem.

Some mention must be made of *colour blindness*. Most local education authorities test for colour vision at the final medical examination; a few test earlier, but almost none do so in the infant school. Work by Waddington (1965) suggests that children with defective colour vision quickly learn to hide this disability. Laughed at for calling the grass red, a child soon learns to call it green, adapting to social pressure. Waddington stressed the anxiety most of the children in her study felt about this defect.

The figures both in this country and the United States suggest that the percentage of colour deficient girls is much smaller than boys; probably five to eight per cent of boys have the defect—some experts placing the figure as high as one in ten. Teachers certainly need to be aware of the importance of this defect since not only do certain innovations in teaching method make extensive use of colour (e.g. signalling devices such as Jones' *Colour Story Reading*, E. and W. Bleasdales' *Reading by Rainbow* and Gattegno's *Words in Colour*—when you see this shape and/or colour pronounce it thus), but the majority of published reading schemes are illustrated in colour and some use colour in the teaching of reading readiness. Teachers may realize that a child is colour blind from the fact that in paintings and drawings people are shown with green hair or animals with green fur, or they may notice that a child cannot choose a brown paint for himself and asks another child to find the 'correct' colour. Colour blind children tend to confuse reds, greens, yellow and brown, and some shades of red are more difficult to distinguish than others.

In discussing the development of orientation, the importance of knowing left from right, and direction generally, has been emphasized. It is not surprising therefore to find that directionability or confusion in direction occurs fairly frequently in the literature on reading backwardness. There is, however, some controversy over the relationship between directionability and what is termed lateral dominance, and it is probably useful to distinguish between the two at this point. *Lateral dominance* refers to the tendency to use one side of the body rather than the other (the superiority of either the right or left hand, eye or foot) in carrying out motor tasks. *Consistent dominance* refers to the preferential use of one hand, eye or foot rather than the other, while *mixed or incomplete dominance* is said to exist when one does not show a consistent preference for one eye, hand or foot. *Crossed dominance* exists when the dominant hand and dominant eye are on opposite sides. Teachers can often observe which is the preferred hand or foot, but usually it is more difficult to obtain information about the dominant eye.

Most teachers will easily observe which are the left-handed children in the class, and in regard to reading progress need to realize that the left-handed child, unless he is a contortionist (which some are), tends to obscure the *series of letters* he is writing as he forms them; his hand and pencil move over the word being written, and not away as is the case with the right-hander. Consequently, the visual feedback he gets from the word as he writes it, is significantly impaired. Some children adopt compensatory postures, but even so, they tend to be more than normally liable to right/left confusions and reversals, since the customary up/down axis of letters is distorted through about 90° in position (the 'Chinese writer' turning the paper sideways and writing down towards the body instead of across it), and as much as 180° in 'the hook' attitude (curling the fist and hand round and above the line being written on and writing from above downwards) where the child is writing with a complete up/down reversal of the ordinary hand/body reference axis. This would help to explain not only the simple right left reversals such as *b* and *d* but also difficulties involved in *p* and *d*, *h* and *y*. If a child has a rather uncertain grasp of letter sequence and also happens to be a left-hander who obscures his work as he writes, one can see how this type of child can be doubly handicapped and his disability tends to have a cumulative effect.

Laterality is the term used to describe awareness of the two sides of the body and the ability to identify them and *directionality* the ability to apply knowledge in everyday activities, such as writing *b* and *d* so they 'face the right way'. It has been suggested that reversal tendencies indicate inadequate development of consistent directionality, and that this in turn is probably related to poorly developed laterality. One can imagine some of the difficulties of left-handed children, and one would expect that both the development of laterality and directionality would be delayed in children of mixed dominance. Work by Cohen and Glass (1968) has established a positive relationship between knowledge of left and right (directionality) and hand dominance. They reported right-handed children were generally more likely to know direction than left- or mixed-handed children. Also, poor readers were more likely to be hesitant or confused in their knowledge of left and right. They observed an age difference as well, the older children being less likely to be confused.

89

With these findings in mind, it would seem advisable for teachers in the infant school to note children's hand preferences, and to watch carefully children who show signs of directional confusion and also exhibit mixed hand dominance. This information should be passed on to the junior schools for these children may developmentally lag behind good readers in the ability to make the directional discriminations so necessary in reading.

Training exercises can be devised by the teacher which may help to develop left to right direction. Tansley (p. 16; 1967) provides some suggestions and it is interesting to note that he emphasizes the importance of speech, children being encouraged to describe their action (e.g. drawing continuous lines between spaces on blackboard or cyclostyled sheets) *as they are carrying them out*: 'now go up, down, to the left, right, etc. ...'. Training exercises of the type used in non-verbal group tests of intelligence or the reading readiness stages of published schemes can be used. They are probably more useful if the pages, exercises or cards are programmed in order of difficulty. Children may have to find the one item 'exactly like' or 'exactly the same' as the first item on the left, or on the card given them by the teacher. The important point is that the child should be able to explain the reasons for his choice and why he rejects the others in the line of figures going left to right, or in the set of cards. Differences in items could involve size and/or colour, rotations and lateral inversions, proceeding from shapes, through letters, to words. In reinforcing left to right progression teachers will soon notice that some children need to start from scratch and others need constant reminders with plenty of practice. It may be useful if the teacher makes two large posters, one with a big arrow pointing right, the other with an arrow pointing left. These can be hung at the front of the room with the right-pointing poster at the right and the other at the left. When children are cutting up old magazines, they can be encouraged to look for people or animals facing left and right and then they can see if they can paste the cut out figures on the appropriate chart.

It should be pointed out that some educationalists (e.g. Cohen and Glass) think that directional confusion possibly may result from generalized emotional confusion on the child's part and that there may be a significant relationship between certain personality variables and directional or dominance factors. On the other hand, difficulties in laterality and directionality tend to be regarded by neurologists and some clinical psychologists as primarily indications of either defect or immaturity in the brain centres.

Neurological dysfunction

Backwardness in reading related to perceptual difficulties may be due to brain damage or delayed development, but it is not easy to discover which condition is operating and therefore which techniques are the most appropriate in the circumstances. It may be that those areas of the brain damaged in some children during the pre-natal period or the birth process, have simply failed to develop in other children. This failure in development may ultimately have to be explained in terms of detailed neuro-chemistry. Some researchers have tried to explain the main features of reading disability in terms of a lack of balance between facilitating and inhibiting chemicals in the brain. Generally, the idea seems to be that reactions (related to cognitive and physical development of the individual resulting from innate and environmental factors) produce a certain chemical. The chemical which cells associated with reading do not share with other cells may fail to be produced or alternatively the reaction may be too fast, so that the cells' growth is affected and they are 'poisoned' or stunted in their growth.

Certainly teachers need to be aware of some of the

types of reading disability attributed to neurological dysfunction. Terms such as *alexia, dyslexia,* and *strephosymbolia,* are used to describe conditions which represent a deviation from the normal pattern of brain organizations. Fernald (1943) has described *alexia* as 'essentially a disorder in the perception or understanding of letter forms, existing apart from any other language or agnostic disturbances'. Sometimes children showing this disability have been described as 'word blind' in the sense that they may be able to see black marks on paper, but are unable to realize that they represent words; i.e. 'blind' to words representing specific sounds and ideas. Alexia is usually associated with brain damage, generally in the left hemisphere. It may be severe or mild. If the part affected is on the dominant side of the brain a group of symptoms known as 'Gerstman's syndrome' may occur, which includes the inability to read as well as difficulty in recognizing objects by touch, confusion in orientation, half vision, inability to write and even to do arithmetic (e.g. seeing 21 for 12).

A mild form of alexia has often been referred to as *dyslexia,* in the sense that where children have failed to profit from reading instruction they have been said to be dyslexic (Money, 1962). The child is unable to read and this failure can be considered quite separately from general cognitive development; i.e. obviously bright and intelligent children may just not be able to 'read'. In the early stages of schooling these children may not easily be detected from the 'slow learner' but their difficulties soon become apparent in the junior school. Reversals and confusions in letters and word forms help to identify this type of child, although this symptom is not peculiar to dyslexia. Other characteristics are oral reading of the 'word pointing' type, and frequent repetitions and guessing of words, often in a particularly soft voice. However, the handwriting of the dyslexic child is often the most distinguishing characteristic; poorly formed letters, unevenness of style, difficulties particularly with *p, g, b, d, q, u, n,* and the printed *t* and *f,* as well as entire words being reversed.

I believe Dr S. T. Orton coined the term 'strephosymbolia' meaning twisted symbols to describe school children who show signs of being confused by the orientation of letters and by whole word methods of teaching. He explained this condition in terms of hemispheral dominance and suggested that the cells of the non-dominant side of the brain form a mirror pattern of the dominant side. Therefore, when this balance is upset, it produces failure to differentiate between letters such as *b* and *d, p* and *q,* etc. Suggested forms of remediation have included greater emphasis on phonic teaching, use of kinesthetic techniques, and emphasis upon the distinguishing features between confusing symbols. However, some educationists seem to consider that the term 'strephosymbolia' covers only some of the aspects of reading disability related to neurological dysfunction.

As can be seen from this brief description, there are possibly two types of 'dyslexic'—(a) with some degree of brain injury characterized by inability to organize sense impressions, memory difficulties, inability to accurately copy complex visual shapes or produce auditory patterns. Such children tend to be clumsy in their movements, impulsive, overactive, and unable to concentrate; (b) no known brain damage but supposed *uneven* brain maturation showing similar symptoms, but also deficiencies which appear in younger children. These children may have members of their families showing these symptoms leading to the inference that an inherited disability is involved. For many teachers it may be difficult to obtain sufficient information about the child's early history and family background to be able to conclude for themselves which type of 'dyslexic' the child may be.

It has been suggested that backward readers should be given 'trial lessons' from which it may be possible to ascertain the nature of their disability, and therefore the most appropriate remedial methods to use. In the light of the discussion in earlier chapters, in cases of dyslexics with marked difficulty in visual perception and analysis, the best method would appear to be the phonic teaching of letter sounds and or spelling patterns and letter 'strings'. When auditory difficulties are apparent, the emphasis may have to be upon the direct association of printed word shapes with their meaning—a much longer and more time consuming approach.

As Vernon (1966) has suggested, the value of supplementary devices must not be forgotten—reading games, workbooks, stories with controlled vocabulary but of older interest appeal. Such devices are essential to arouse and maintain the desire to learn to read in these children who may have experienced little but frustration in their contacts with reading.

If school records have been adequately kept, it should be possible for teachers of older backward readers to be able to find out whether causal factors are mainly in the educational area; i.e. history of inadequate or inappropriate teaching methods and materials. If this is so, it is a case of finding out what are the particular reading skills that are weakest and developing these. Where, however, this can be ruled out, emotional and/or neurological disorders are probably the causal factors and depending on the severity of the handicap, reading progress may be slow or even non-existent. For these children, teachers need to realize that a long period of individual remedial teaching may be necessary for them to make any improvement.

Anxiety and reading

As it was necessary to distinguish between types of dyslexics, so one must distinguish between those backward readers whose disability has been caused primarily by emotional disturbance, and those who have become in-creasingly anxious and worried by their failure to learn to read. Some researchers have found a relationship between reading difficulties and the emotional atmosphere of the home (e.g. Pringle et al., 1966). It may be that the home is too demanding, possibly the mother over-protective and the child cannot persevere in the face of difficulties or, alternatively, parents are not interested in the child's school work or are not achievement orientated. Some children may need reassurance from the teacher that they can and should learn to read.

However, it cannot be assumed that all anxious children will fail to progress in reading. It seems that some anxious children seek a refuge from their day-to-day worries in the ability to read, finding emotional satisfaction in an escape from reality. It may very well depend upon the child's level of intelligence. The less intelligent child is more likely to find reading a source of further worry than an escape from their anxieties. Also, some of the evidence suggests that the school's atmosphere may have some effect, choice of instructional methods making a consider-able difference for certain kinds of pupils. For instance, intelligent children with a high degree of anxiety may make better progress in a structured environment involving some-what formal ways of teaching, which include phonics.

Also, in the context of anxiety one should consider the sex of the child. Research shows that boys are generally less anxious in the school setting and certainly less willing to conform to the demands of the school situation. Backward boy readers may not be as anxious about their reading failure as their teachers suppose.

Sex differences

Consistently throughout the research reports of reading surveys, one finds the proportion of two poor boy readers to every girl (e.g. latest Inner London Education Authority survey 1969: 20·9 per cent boys were poor readers compared to 10 per cent girls; 31,308 eight-year-olds tested). Some researchers have found that girls' superiority is more marked at the lower level of reading ability, the spread of raw scores for boys on tests of reading attainment being wider than that of girls; i.e. there are more very good and very poor readers amongst boys whereas the girls are less differentiated. Certainly this same trend is apparent in relation to teachers' assessments of boys and girls, teachers making a more general evaluation of girls than boys, their ratings of boys being more likely to vary according to the apparent possibilities and limitations of the child's home.

It is usually claimed that boys mature physically at a slower rate than girls, and if mental development accompanies physical development then the teacher of young children might *expect* that more boys than girls in her class would have difficulty in learning to read.

In regard to boys' reading attainment, social and environmental factors are probaby very important in determining and emphasizing the differences in early perceptual development which exist between the sexes. However, teachers' expectations about boys may be a crucial factor in the teaching situation. Moore (1967) has outlined a theory which links early speech development to the typical interests and identifications of boys and girls. His finding that on average, girls talk earlier than boys appears to be confirmed by the National Child Development Study (Pringle et al., 1966). Moore found that girls' language development was more constant than that of boys, and although the girls showed early verbal superiority, by school age the boys had caught up. Moore also cites recent experimental work which indicated that baby girls learned to respond to *auditory* and boys to *visual* stimuli. This could be due to sex differences in sensitivity or in the 'natural' differences between the sexes. If indeed girl babies have greater auditory sensitivity from an earlier age, this could be an asset at the time of learning to talk. Certainly girl toddlers imitate their mothers and seek their companionship and therefore are more likely to hear and copy adult speech. Subsequently they bring to the 'reading readiness' stage not only a higher level of speech development but probably superior auditory abilities.

Pringle (1966) reported girls as superior to boys in regard to mispronounced words, suggesting that boys may not listen as carefully as girls or may have inferior auditory acuity at that age. A much earlier study by Henry (1947) of six- to twelve-year-olds reported high-frequency hearing loss as being significantly more frequent among boys, and if one recalls the sequence in which children learn to respond to pitch, then this could be interpreted as evidence of boys' later auditory development. Thackray (1965) using an American reading readiness test with English children found significant sex differences in favour of girls on the auditory but not the visual sub-tests.

Of equal importance at the beginning reading stage are motivational factors, and there is quite a lot of evidence which suggests that boys are less likely to have favourable attitudes towards school and learning, and that it may be more difficult to secure their interest and co-operation. Boys tend to be more aggressive (Pringle et al., 1966) and therefore may, be difficult to teach. Certainly research suggests that boys are less concerned with pleasing the teacher than with the values and approval of their classmates. Girls tend to perceive their teachers' feelings towards them more favourably, and teachers' behaviour ratings of girls are in fact generally more favourable.

McNeil (1964) put to the test his suggestion that boys would progress better under the 'neutral' conditions of programmed instruction, and he found this so in an experiment with boy beginners. However, in the next class, when these children were taught once more by women teachers, they failed to make progress. Information from the children and their teachers suggested that the children received differential treatment—boys being 'ticked-off' more by their teachers, and given fewer opportunities to read. NcNeil's research design has been criticized, but experiments such as this may provide evidence that the school procedures of many teachers in the early stages of schooling, practically all of whom are women, conflict more with the personality traits of boys than girls. My own opinion is that the heavy reliance by teachers upon the sentence or 'look-and-say' methods as beginning methods, may be a mistake for some boys. Boys' constructive interests may be aroused by the use of synthetic methods (e.g. phonics—'word building') where their auditory development is sufficiently developed, or where this is still weak, linguistic methods emphasizing spelling patterns may appeal. These methods offer a method of 'unlocking' unfamiliar words and appeal to the 'masculine' desire to know how a thing works, as well as providing a valued measure of independence.

When one considers that some published reading materials in schools are more appropriate to girls' interests, one might be tempted to wonder how so many boys progress as rapidly as they do. Research has suggested that boys prefer non-fiction, and adventurous and historical themes, while girls prefer fairy tales, myths, fantasy and stories of family life, i.e. development of personal relationships. The content of beginning readers emphasizes family relationships and when the vocabulary is expanded and stories included use simplified versions of fairy tales and folk tales, rarely including the more robust legends which would appeal to boys. And what of the way in which boys are presented in these early reading books? A study of American schemes concluded that generally the differences between the roles of boys and girls were not emphasized, the children's activities were usually more appropriate to girls, and activities begun by boys were more likely to end in failure!

Discussions with experienced teachers suggests that competitive games for word and sound learning are useful for boys, e.g. word lotto, fishing games, Junior scrabble; 'home-made' books about their own interests and activities; instructions for using building and construction games, and published series such as Ginn's *Active Reading Series* and E. J. Arnold's *Dragon Books and Cowboy Sam Series*, the *Space Books* by Wheaton, any of the *Doctor Seuss* books (Collins) and Oxford University Press *Oxford Colour Reading Books*.

Hearing-impaired children

Boys' auditory abilities may develop more slowly than girls' and create specific difficulties for them, but they are as nothing compared to the child who has suffered significant hearing impairment before school age. As Johnson (1962) has pointed out 'retardation in reading ability ... is a particular characteristic of children with impaired hearing in ordinary schools', but it does not follow that children with the severest hearing impairment are the most backward in reading. What is important is when the impairment occurred in regard to the acquisition of speech.

Children with impaired hearing are widely scattered in ordinary schools so it is rare for teachers to have much experience of their characteristics and needs. Certainly, where a child is backward in reading and language development is slow, it would be wise to consider a test of hearing. A family history of deafness, siblings with hearing impairment, difficulties in hearing fine sound discriminations as between similar sounding letters, withdrawn behaviour or exceptional shyness, or difficulties in following verbal instructions may be symptoms of undetected hearing loss.

Where impairment has been ascertained, it would be

advisable if at all possible for the teacher to try and find out in what way this impairment is likely to produce problems, particularly in regard to learning to read. Certainly the teacher can make allowance for the way in which these children seem to hear better on some occasions rather than others. Factors affecting this can be the noise level in the classroom, the distance between the child and teacher; the child's ability to lip read and his opportunity of seeing the teacher's mouth; the teacher's fatigue level and how this affects the pitch of her voice; the teacher's use of facial gestures, etc. To provide a child with a favourable seating position may not be easy, especially in the less formal classroom setting, so on occasion, it may be necessary for the teacher to give individual instructions or make sure the particular child is watching her.

Where a child wears a hearing aid, the attitude of both teacher and class can be important. If this is accepted as nothing out of the ordinary, the hearing-impaired child will not be tempted to misuse or neglect their aid. Also, it is necessary for the teacher to have some knowledge of possible simple faults which occur and how to remedy them. For instance, a loosely fitting ear mould can cause a whistling noise; an aid may not work because the battery has gone or the cord needs attention; the aid may be clipped in an unsuitable place.

However, even with the use of a powerful hearing aid, the heard pattern of words will remain incomplete or confusing for some of these children. For them, the written pattern is the only generally acceptable version of language which can be fully understood. Fluency in reading can however provide them with access to the ideas of books and written communication generally, and so enable them, particularly when schooling is completed, to remain truly in contact with events and the means to continue learning.

The popular published reading schemes are rarely suitable for these children, and teachers may need to rely on individual methods using the child's particular interests to create active learning situations in which the children can handle concrete materials and relate written word patterns to what they are doing, part-hearing and lip reading. Hand made reading materials then need to be made using vocabulary thus acquired. G. W. Redgate in an article 'Reading for Deaf Children', *U.K.R.A. Bulletin* No. 4 (Dec.), 1965, explains this process in greater detail, but at the present time there seems a pressing need for further research and particularly innovation in regard to the specific reading needs of these children.

Disadvantaged children

Another group of children who may demand special attention are those children coming from homes in which reading is an under-valued skill. Variously called the 'disadvantaged', 'culturally deprived' or 'underprivileged', research suggests that these children are exclusive neither to any one race nor to one locality but generally tend to exist in overcrowded, urban conditions. The father is often absent from home or when present follows a semi-skilled or unskilled occupation and the sub-culture of the home is such that reading is not a skill which offers great rewards. From an early age children in this setting are likely to have experienced both sensory and language deprivation. Parents of such children may fail to provide the 'corrective feedback' in language to which middle-class children are accustomed from an early age. In Bernstein's terms their language structure tends to be restricted rather than elaborated.

With this type of developmental background, these children often appear unfamiliar with the content and vocabulary of the popular published reading schemes. Their language structure is such that they find it difficult to abstract information, to seriate and classify, and therefore to readily grasp not only the idea of such things as phonic generalizations or 'rules' but also to understand abstract concepts met in reading such as 'zoo' or 'library'. Concepts such as these involve ideas not readily understood or further classifications and abstractions; e.g. the difference between 'wild' and 'tame' in connection with 'zoos'.

Overcrowded conditions are likely to affect their listening ability, so that not only do they have considerable difficulty in discriminating between similar sounds (e.g. 'fine' as against 'gross' discriminations), but as their teachers sometimes mention, they can 'tune me out at will'. Teachers also comment that they can recall facts or insignificant details, but often have considerable difficulty in remembering the sequence of a story or making inferences about what might have happened before or after events in a picture.

Research suggests that these children respond well when the following conditions exist. They are often told how they are getting on and assured that progress is being made; they are set short-range objectives which can be accomplished in a reasonably short time; they are able to use concrete materials or allowed to mime or act out abstract concepts; they are given tangible rewards as well as verbal praise and reassurances.

Games would be a practical and effective way of teaching some of the reading skills to these children. Unfortunately, the choice in published reading games is limited at the present time, there being few variations on the Bingo and Lotto principle. However, teachers are ever resourceful and can often see how popular published games can be used to develop particular reading skills. The main difficulty in reading materials seems to be how to ensure that these children are not only able to obtain books whose content are of interest, but books whose vocabulary and language structure are not too unfamiliar. The danger exists that these children will look at the pictures in the books in the reading corner but fail to reach the stage of being 'hooked' by reading. It is advisable for the teacher to try to grade reading materials, allowing these children a choice between books of equivalent reading difficulty. However, assessing the reading level of books is not an easy task. Reading ability formulas can be used but these are time consuming and publishers' ratings in their catalogues are not reliable as they are rarely based on valid methods of evaluation. The 'cloze' procedure may eventually prove to be an easier measure of 'readability' levels.

Sometimes teachers can find a published reading scheme with a high level of repetition and supplementary books based on this restricted vocabulary. Similarly, letter-sound control rather than vocabulary control may be a useful alternative; e.g. the linguistic type of reader in which the introduction of different letter sounds is controlled. 'Signalling devices' may be useful with these children as they help to simplify the beginning stage and emphasize the 'decoding' aspect of reading. Once this is established, wider reading may enlarge their vocabulary. However, the use of i.t.a or 'signalling devices' involving fine discriminations in colour or shapes may necessitate considerable preparation at the visual discrimination stage and checking of the development of the stages of growth from gross to fine discrimination.

Assuring these children about their progress means that their teachers may have to rethink their teaching aims, so that they break up the reading process into smaller units or chunks of learning. Also, this process may necessitate the keeping of much more detailed records as well as the carrying out of more frequent checks on individual children's progress.

Atypical learners

Some of the 'disadvantaged' children will be slow learners in the sense that their rate of progress will be related to the level of their inherited ability. Some of them will be of subnormal intelligence. Generally, it is considered that such children are not incapable of learning to read, but inevitably the process will take longer and it may not be completed by the end of compulsory schooling. Such children require more pre-reading experience, especially in regard to the use of language. When they do begin, they probably need slower and more gradual teaching and there may always be difficulty in the understanding of the meaning of words in comparison with the ability to recognize words. Also, it is well to bear in mind that the slow learner usually requires a greater variety of activities over a longer period of time than is usually the case for the 'average' pupil.

Most of the well-known text books on reading have a section on the needs of the slow-learning pupils, so as space is limited, I should like to concentrate instead on the equally atypical pupil, the 'gifted' or 'advantaged' children since until recently far less attention had been given to their needs. Often it was considered that these children 'taught' themselves and therefore did not constitute a problem to the teacher (Austin et al., 1964, reported that in 19 out of 51 school systems in the United States, the bright readers in the classrooms received the *least* instructional emphasis).

The above-average child may be identified on the basis of group intelligence or attainment tests, but the astute and experienced teacher can also pick them out using their own informal observations. These children often excel at memory games, have an extensive vocabulary and use words imaginatively. At an abstract level they can generalize and recognize relationships. Curious about many things, they can follow elaborate oral directions and their pictures and stories show considerable detail. They are rarely physical or social misfits.

In studies of gifted children, Witty (1969) found that most of the children came from homes in which abundant opportunities were given in their early years for sensory-motor and perceptual learning and for first-hand exploration of the environment. Indeed some educationalists contend that giftedness is largely a product of a favourable collection of environmental conditions. Certainly Durkin's studies of children who learned to read early showed that the parents of early readers were characterized as having respect for learning and encouraging it in their children. Witty found similar results regarding parental attitudes in his studies of gifted children who read early. Parents read often to their children and answered questions patiently and fully. Although they did not put pressure on their children to learn to read, they made a point of providing an assortment of books and magazines, alphabet and number books, dictionaries, easy-to-read books, encyclopaedias, children's magazines and story books of many kinds. Cappa and Shubert (1962) also found in their group of gifted children that the parents had assumed considerable responsibility for extending their children's reading skills by purchasing books, giving them magazine subscriptions, providing a place and time for their reading in the home and general encouragement of both the quality and the quantity of home reading.

Some educationalists advocate using the best of the published reading schemes and individualized reading approaches in teaching these children. For instance, Benson (1967) maintains that reading instruction and materials for the gifted and average differ little in kind. 'The differences, if any, lie in providing a greater range and level of difficulty of materials.' However, if these children are to be given more difficult reading material, they should also be given help in the difficulties they will encounter, e.g. instruction in how to use indexes, tables of content, and other aids in locating information on topics of interest to them. Probably they also need guidance in critical and creative reading skills since their powers to do logical and critical thinking may become much greater than the average pupil's. Teachers of gifted children need to act as guides and not as final authorities. In this capacity, they can allow the gifted child to gain his own knowledge and time for practice and experimentation. They can show him how to make and test informed guesses, and ask him to translate, interpret, summarize and apply his new information. Many of these pupils enjoy the challenge of locating words, learning about their historical development, and ascertaining their various meanings. Books such as Helene and Charlton Laird's *Tree of Language* (Faber, 1957), Basil Cottle's *The Penguin Dictionary of Surnames* (Penguin, 1967), or even the Opies *The Lore and Language of Schoolchildren* can provide entertainment and enlightenment.

Fast readers can be encouraged to prepare oral or written book reports, which include evaluative comments on the book's qualities. This work can be developed into analysis of fictional characters' motives, evaluation of plot development, and study of the author's purpose, style, and personality. Pupils can be asked to compare two different newspaper articles dealing with the same topic, or a biography and a fictionalized story about a famous individual.

Geboe (1960) found that a programme of folklore reading could be effective for superior readers of the Junior age level. Common themes can be traced in fairy tales, fables and legends. Also, these advanced readers can be encouraged to share their interest and their discoveries with their classmates through dramatizations, puppet plays, stories illustrated with the use of the flannel or cellograph board, or tape recorded book reports or discussions, e.g.

book characters identified by their descriptions or reported speech.

These children may, however, need some help with their spelling for a certain period. Pleassas and Dison (1965) have suggested that they need to have their attention drawn to 'the visual study of words and to the spelling relationship between words and their derived and compound forms'. From their reading they can form phonetic generalizations which tend to be logical but not valid for English usage, so that they are surprised by the 'exceptions' which occur to the 'phonic rules' they have generalized for themselves.

Conclusion

In this last chapter I have tried to identify certain types of children with particular needs. The list is not complete, but alas limitations of space necessitate some omissions. The immigrant child with his special language forms or speech patterns, the absent child who may have been away when a particular reading skill was treated briefly in a group lesson, the child whose birth date is such that he has had a shorter period of infant schooling to others in his class—come to mind as children likely to experience difficulty.

It is impossible to remove completely the element of anxiety from the learning situation. Some educationalists would argue that even if it were possible, it would not be desirable. Certainly though, the teacher should be able to recognize signs of stress in individual children and, as a consequence, adjust the learning situation for them. It is the experienced teacher who understands not only the psychological and cognitive needs of her children but also knows what children must learn, when they are undertaking that long and complex task—learning to read, the key to so much!

Bibliography

AMES, L. B. et al. (1953), 'Development of perception in the young child as observed in responses to the Rorschach Test Blots', *Journal of Genetic Psychology*, 82, 183.

AMES, L. B. and WALKER, R. N. (1964), 'Prediction of later reading ability from Kindergarten Rorschach and I.Q. scores', *Journal Educational Psychology*, 55, 300-13.

AUSTIN, M. C. and MORRISON, C. (1963), *The First R—The Harvard Report on Reading in the Elementary Schools*, New York: Macmillan.

BAILEY, M. H. (1967), 'The utility of phonic generalizations in Grades One through Six', *Reading Teacher*, 20, 413-18.

BENSON, J. T. (1967), 'Materials of instruction for the socially atypical child ... advantaged', in D. L. Clealand and P. E. Stanton (eds.) *Reading in its Sociological Setting*, a report of the twenty-third annual conference and course on reading. Pittsburg Pa.: University of Pittsburg Press.

BIEMILLER, A. J. (1968), 'Patterns of Changes in Oral Reading Errors During the First Grade', Unpublished paper, Cornell University, Ithaca, N.Y.

BOND, G. L. and DYKSTRA, R. (1967), *Report of the Co-ordinating Center for First Grade Reading Instruction Programs*, Minneapolis: University of Minnesota.

BORMUTH, J. R. (1964), *Relationships between Selected Language Variables and Comprehension Ability and Difficulty*, U.S. Office of Education Co-operative Research Project No. 2082, Los Angeles: University of California.

BROWN, R. and BELLUGI, V. (1964), 'Three processes in the

child's acquisition of syntax', *Harvard Educational Review*, 34 (Spring), 133-51.

BRUCE, D. J. (1964), 'The analysis of word sounds by young children', *British Journal of Educational Psychology*, 34, p. 158-70.

BRUNER, J. S. (1960), *The Process of Education*, New York: Vintage Books.

CAPPA, D. and SHUBERT, D. G. (1962), 'Do parents help gifted children read?' *Journal of Educational Research*, 56 (1), 33-6.

CHALL, J. (1958), *Readability: An Appraisal of Research and Application*, Bureau of Educational Research, Ohio State University.

CHALL, J. (1963), 'Auditory blending ability: a factor in success in beginning reading', *Reading Teacher*, 17, 113-18.

CHALL, J. (1967), *Learning to Read—the Great Debate*, New York: McGraw-Hill.

CHALL, J. (1969), 'Research in linguistics and reading instruction: implications for further research and practice' in J. A. Figurel (ed.) *Reading and Realism*, Vol. 13 (1) Proceedings of the thirteenth annual convention, International Reading Association, 560-71.

CHOMSKY, N. and HALLE, M. (1968), *Sound Pattern of English*, New York: Harper and Row.

CHRISTENSON, A. (1969), 'Oral reading errors of intermediate grade children at their independent, instructional, and frustration reading levels' in J. A. Figurel (ed.) *Reading and Realism*, I.R.A., 674-7.

CLAY, M. M. (1966), 'Emergent Reading Behaviour', Unpublished doctoral dissertation, University of Auckland, New Zealand.

CLAY, M. (1969), 'Reading errors and self-correction behaviour' *British Journal of Educational Psychology*, 39 (1), 47-56.

CLYMER, T. (1963), 'The Utility of Phonic Generalizations in the Primary Grades', *Reading Teacher*, 16, 252-8.

COHEN, A. and GLASS, G. (1968), 'Lateral dominance and reading ability', *Reading Teacher*, 21, 343-8.

DAVIDSON, H. P. (1931), 'An experimental study of bright, average and dull children at the four-year mental level', *Genetic Psychology Monograph* 9, 119-289.

DEIGHTON, L. C. (1959), *Vocabulary Development in the Classroom*, New York Bureau of Publications, Teachers College, Columbia University.

DIACK, H. (1965), *In Spite of the Alphabet*, Chatto and Windus.

DOWNING, J. (1969), 'How children think about reading', *Reading Teacher*, 23, 217-30.

DURKIN, D. (1964), 'Early readers—reflections after six years of research', *Reading Teacher*, 18, 3-7.

DURRELL, D. (1968), 'Phonics problems in beginning reading' in *Forging Ahead in Reading*, Vol. 12 (1) 12th Annual Convention, I.R.A., 19-25.

ELKIND, D. and WEISS, J. (1967), 'Studies in perceptual development III: perceptual exploration', *Child Development*, 38, 553-61.

ELKONIN, D. B. (1963), 'The psychology of mastering the elements of reading' in Brian and Joan Simon (eds.) *Educational Psychology in the U.S.S.R.*, Stanford, Calif.: Stanford University Press, 165-79.

FERNALD, G. M. (1943), *Remedial Techniques in Basic School Subjects*, New York, McGraw-Hill.

FLESCH, R. (1955), *Why Johnny Can't Read*, New York: Harper.

FOWLER, W. (1962), 'Teaching a two-year-old to read: An experiment in early childhood learning', *Genetic Psychology Monograph*, 116, 181-283.

GATES, A. I. (1937), 'The necessary mental age for beginning reading', *Elementary School Journal*, 37, 497-508.

GEBOE, J. (1960), 'Folklore for superior readers in the third grade', *Elementary English*, 37, 93-7.

GIBSON, E. J. et al. (1962), 'A developmental study of the discrimination of letter-like forms', *Journal comparative Physiol. Psychol.*, 55, 897-906.

GOINS, J. T. (1958), 'Visual perceptual abilities and early reading progress', *Supplementary Educational Monograph*, No. 87.

GOLDMAN, R. J. (1957), 'Learning and Growth' in *Learning: In School and Society*. Papers: University of Birmingham Institute of Education Summer School, 69-96.

GOODACRE, E. J. (1969), 'Published reading schemes', *Educational Research*, 12 (1), 30-5.

GOODMAN, K. S. (1969), 'Analysis of oral reading miscues: applied psycholinguistics', *Reading Research Quarterly*, 9-30.

GOTTSCHALK, J. et al (1964), 'Spatial organisation of children's responses to a pictorial display', *Child Development*, 37, 811-15.

HARRELL, L. (1957), 'A comparison of the development of oral and written language in school-age children', *Monograph Society for Research in Child Development*, 22 (3), Serial No. 66.

HAY, J. and WINGO, C. E. (1948), *Reading with Phonics*, New York: J. B. Lippincott.

HENRY, S. (1947), 'Children's audiograms in relation to reading achievement', *Journal of Genetic Psychology*, 70, 211-31; 71, 3-48 and 49-63.

HILLERICH, R. L. (1967), 'What's one way to teach beginning reading', in R. Molony (ed.) *Reading: Research to Reality*, California Reading Association, 36-54.

JOHNSON, J. C. (1962), *'Educating Hearing-Impaired Children in Ordinary Schools*, Manchester University Press.

KAGAN, J. (1965), 'Reflection-impulsivity and reading ability', *Child Development*, 36, 609.

LABOV, W. (1967), 'Some sources of reading problems for Negro Speakers of Non-Standard English', in A. Frazier (ed.) *New Directions in Elementary English*, Champaign, Ill. N.C.T.E.

LEE, D. M. and ALLEN, R. V. (1963), *Learning to Read Through Experience*, New York: Appleton-Century-Croft, Inc.

LEVIN, H. (1964-67), *Project Literacy Reports*, Nos. 1-8, Ithaca, New York: Cornell University.

LYNN, R. (1963), 'Reading readiness II—Reading readiness and the perceptual abilities of young children, *Educational Research*, 6, 10-15.

BIBLIOGRAPHY

MACKINNON, A. R. (1959), *How Children Learn to Read*, Toronto: Copp Clark Publishing Co.

MARCHBANKS, G. and LEVIN, H. (1965), 'Cues by which children recognise words', *Journal Educational Psychology*, 106, 57-61.

MARQUARDT, W. F. (1964), 'Language interference in reading', *Reading Teacher*, 18, 214-18.

MARSHALL, S. (1963), *An Experiment in Education*, Cambridge University Press.

MASON, G. E. (1967), 'Pre-schoolers' concepts of reading', *Reading Teacher*, 21, 130-7.

MCCULLOUGH, C. (1968), 'Balanced reading development' in *Innovation and Change in Reading Instruction*, 67th Yearbook, Nat. Soc. Study of Educ., II, 320-56.

MCNEIL, J. D. (1964), 'Programmed instruction versus classroom procedures in teaching boys to read', *American Educational Research Journal*, 1, 113-19.

MONEY, J. ed. (1962), *Reading Disability: Progress and Research Needs in Dyslexia*, Baltimore: John Hopkins Press.

MOORE, T. (1967), 'Language and intelligence: a longitudinal study of the first eight years', *Human Development*, 10, 88-106.

MORPHETT, M. V. and WASHBURNE, C. (1931), 'When Should Children Begin to Learn to Read?' *Elementary School Journal*, 31, 496-503.

MUEHL, S. (1962), 'The effects of letter-name knowledge on learning to read a word list in kindergarten children', *Journal of Educational Psychology* (Aug.), 181-6.

O'CONNOR, R. and HERMELIN, B. (1961), 'Like and cross modality recognition in subnormal children', *Quarterly Journal of Experimental Psychology*, 13, 48.

OLMSTEAD, D. L. (1966), 'A theory of the child's learning of phonology', *Language*, 42, 531-5.

ORPHET, R. E. et al. (1966), 'Relation between Fifth Grade Achievement and Differential Abilities—Tested in Kindergarten', paper read at the California Assoc. of School Psychometrists and Psychologists, Los Angeles (March).

PIAGET, J. and INHELDER, B. (1948), *Le Representation de*

l'Espace Chez L'Enfant, Paris: Presses Universitaires de France.

PLEASSAS, G. P. and DISON, P. A. (1965), 'Spelling performance of good readers', *California Journal of Educ. Res.*, 16, 14-22.

PLEASSAS, G. P. and OAKES, C. R. (1964), 'Prereading experiences of selected early readers', *Reading Teacher*, 17, 241-5.

POOLE, I. (1934), 'Genetic development of articulation of consonant sounds in speech', *Elementary English Review*, 2, 159-61.

POPP, H. M. (1964), 'Visual discrimination of alphabet letters', *Reading Teacher*, 17, 221-5.

PRINGLE, M. L. et al. (1966), *11,000 Seven-year-olds*, Longmans Green.

REICHARD, S. et al. (1944), 'The development of concept formation in children', *American Journal of Orthopsychiatry*, 14, 156.

REID, J. F. (1966), 'Learning to think about reading', *Educational Research*, 9 (1), 56-62.

ROBERTS, G. R. (1969), *Reading in Primary Schools*, Routledge & Kegan Paul.

SHUBERT, D. G. and WALTON, H. T. (1968), 'Effects of induced astigmatism', *Reading Teacher*, 21, 547-51.

SIMS, N. and WILLIAMS, P. (1969), 'The development of phonic skills in infant school children—a preliminary study' in *Children at Risk*, University of Swansea, Department of Education, Schools Council Research Project in Compensatory Education.

SPACHE, G. D. (1968), 'Contributions of allied fields to the teaching of reading' in *Innovation and Change in Reading*, 67th Yearbook, N.S.S.E., II, 237-90.

SUTON, M. H. (1964), 'Readiness for reading at the kindergarten level', *Reading Teacher*, 17, 234-9.

TANSLEY, A. E. (1967), *Reading and Remedial Reading*, Routledge & Kegan Paul.

TEEGARDEN, L. (1933), 'Tests for the tendency to reversals in reading', *Journal of Educational Research*, 27, 81-97.

TEMPLIN, M. C. (1957), *Certain Language Skills in Children*, *their Development and Interrelationship*, Minneapolis: University of Minnesota Press.

THACKRAY, D. V. (1965), 'The relationship between reading readiness and reading progress', *British Journal of Educational Psychology*, 35, 252-4.

VENEZKY, R. L. and WEIR, R. H. (1966), *A Study of Selected Spelling to Sound Correspondence Patterns*, Co-operative Research Project, Stanford University.

VERNON, M. D. (1966), 'Research on backwardness in reading', *First International Reading Symposium* (Oxford), 148-59.

VERNON, M. D. (1966), 'Perception in relation to cognition' in A. J. Kidd and J. L. Rivoire (eds.) *Perceptual Development in Children*, University of London Press, 391-406.

WADDINGTON, M. (1965), 'Colour Blindness in Young Children', *Educational Research*, 7, (3), 236-40.

WEBSTER, J. (1967), *Reading Failure*, Boston/Mass.: Ginn.

WEPMAN, J. M. (1960), 'Auditory discrimination, speech and reading', *Elementary School Journal*, 60, 325-33.

WHEELOCK, W. H. and SILVAROLI, N. M. (1967), 'An investigation of visual discrimination training for beginning readers', *Journal of Typographic Research*, 1, 147-56.

WITKIN, H. A. et al. (1962) *Psychological Differentiation: Studies of Development*, New York: Wiley.

WITTY, P. A. (1969), 'Reading for the Gifted' in *Reading and Realism*, I.R.A., 47-55.

WOLF et al. (1967), *Critical Reading Ability of Elementary School Children*, Report of Project No. 5. 1040 Washington D.C.: Office of Education.

Suggestions for further reading

Where is reading research reported?

British Publications

The two major academic journals in this country to regularly report reading research are the *British Journal of Educational Psychology* and *Educational Research*. Other publications such as *English in Education, Remedial Education* and *The School Librarian* sometimes include articles on reading research or review articles and books published on the subject of children's reading. The journal of the United Kingdom Reading Association (UKRA) called *Reading* deals solely with the subject of reading research and also includes reviews of books, materials and apparatus. The Association also plan to issue regularly monographs written in a readable style on various topics of interest to teachers of reading.

American Publications

The International Reading Association (IRA) has produced a very useful annotated bibliography *Sources of Reading Research*, which covers the standard references, journals and periodicals, bibliographies and summaries dealing with different aspects of reading research. The libraries of many of our Institutes and Colleges of Education subscribe to certain of these American journals and periodicals. IRA itself produces journals for its members which cater for different readerships; e.g. *The Reading Teacher* (elementary or primary level); *Journal of Reading* (High School and College/secondary and adult); *Reading Research Quarterly* (more scholarly publication concerned mainly with experimental research and theoretical speculation).

A useful feature of some of these American publications has been the practice of regularly devoting a particular issue to summarizing the reading research of the previous year. Until 1966, the February issue of *The Reading Teacher* carried an annual survey of reading research. Since then the summary has appeared in the winter issue of the *Reading Research Quarterly*. The *Journal of Educational Research* also devotes an issue (February, sometimes March) to a detailed survey of the findings and conclusions of the previous year's research.

Another means of making research results available to the classroom teacher is to improve the means of collating and disseminating research information. In the United States this work is carried out by ERIC/CRIER. The letters ERIC stand for Educational Resources and Information Centre, a nationwide, comprehensive information system based on computer facilities. Eighteen clearinghouses throughout the United States send information to the central ERIC at Washington; the clearinghouse devoted to reading research information being jointly run by Indiana University and the IRA. (CRIER stands for Clearinghouse on Retrieval of Information and the Evaluation of Reading.) ERIC/CRIER obtains research reports, materials, etc. related to all aspects of reading behaviour and evaluates, abstracts, and stores this information in such a way that it can be easily retrieved and disseminated. ERIC/CRIER has undertaken information analysis activities which have produced guides to information sources in reading, state-of-the-art monographs, special bibliographies and reviews, basic reference lists, and broad subject bibliographies. These items can be obtained either in hard-cover or inexpensively on microfiche which needs a microfilm reader. ERIC/CRIER produce a brochure *Reading Resources for the 70's* which lists their various productions in detail.

Addresses

United Kingdom Reading Association—further information from Dr E. J. Goodacre, c/o Psychology Department, Institute of Education, University of London, Malet Street, London W.1.

International Reading Association—Six Tyre Avenue, Newark, Del. 19711.

ERIC/CRIER—200 Pine Hall, School of Education, Indiana University, Bloomington, Indiana 47401.

For Product Safety Concerns and Information please contact our EU
representative GPSR@taylorandfrancis.com Taylor & Francis Verlag GmbH,
Kaufingerstraße 24, 80331 München, Germany

Batch number: 08153778

Printed by Printforce, the Netherlands